BERTOLT BRECHT

The Caucasian Chalk Circle

Notes and questions by
Ray Speakman

Heinemann Educational
a division of Heinemann Publishers (Oxford) Ltd

Halley Court, Jordan Hill, Oxford OX2 8EJ

OXFORD LONDON EDINBURGH
MADRID ATHENS BOLOGNA PARIS
MELBOURNE SYDNEY AUCKLAND SINGAPORE TOKYO
IBADAN NAIROBI HARARE GABORONE PORTSMOUTH NH (USA)

This translation of *The Caucasian Chalk Circle* first published in 1960 by Methuen
and Co. and in the present revised version in 1976 by
Eyre Methuen in Volume 7 of Brecht's *Collected Plays*.
Hereford edition first published by Heinemann/Methuen 1989.
Heinemann Play edition first published 1996.

Translation copyright © 1976 by Stefan S. Brecht.
Original work entitled *Der Kaukasische Kreidekreis*.
Copyright © 1955 by Suhrkamp Verlag, Berlin.

Introduction and notes in this edition copyright © Ray Speakman 1989.

10 9 8 7 6 5 4 3 2 1

00 99 98 97 96

A catalogue record for this book is available from the British Library on request.

ISBN 0 435 23317 3

Cover design by Keith Pointing

Original design by Jeffery White Creative Associates

Typeset by Books Unlimited (Nottm)

Printed by Clays Ltd, St Ives plc

CONTENTS

PREFACE

In this edition of *The Caucasian Chalk Circle*, you will find notes, questions and activities to help in studying the play in class.

The introduction provides background information on the author and on the social context of the play.

The activities at the end of the book range from straightforward *Keeping Track* questions which can be tackled at the end of each scene to focus close attention on what is happening in the play, to more detailed work on character, performance, themes and criticism in the *Explorations* sections.

If you are already using the Hereford edition of *The Caucasian Chalk Circle*, you will find that the page numbering in the actual playscript is the same, allowing the two editions to be easily used side by side.

INTRODUCTION

Bertolt Brecht was born in Germany in 1898 and died in 1956. He survived two world wars, the rise of Hitler, exile in Scandinavia and the USA, questioning by the House Committee on Unamerican Activities and the division of Europe, particularly Berlin, into 'east' and 'west'. Throughout this period of political, economic and social change, and on to the present day, Brecht's work had and has enormous influence.

Brecht believed that theatre should have a social function. Whilst entertaining it should also educate its audience. An earlier German dramatist, Schiller, wrote in 1795:

> *The theatre is the establishment where entertainment is united with instruction, rest with exertion, pastime with education.*

This is a succinct description both of Brecht's philosophy of theatre and of his play, *The Caucasian Chalk Circle*.

The play was written in 1944; Hitler was on the edge of defeat and Brecht, like many others, was looking towards the future postwar world. For Brecht the future was communism. The play opens in the USSR and the first scene shows communism as a system in which justice is achieved through rational discussion among the workers of two collective farms. Elsewhere in the play justice and truth are seen in conflict under the 'old' political system of laws designed to maintain a self-seeking minority. The 'moral' of the play is that rights are not inherited, but earned. Expressed thus, the play may seem over-simple, even naive. It is neither, it is a complex and challenging piece of work which the student will find, as Brecht intended, entertaining and stimulating.

The **Questions and Explorations** which follow the text are intended to promote a close reading of the play and a considered response to it. The shorter questions should help the student articulate his or her thoughts during a first reading, and the longer assignments encourage detailed pieces of GCSE coursework or examination preparation for A level. The approach suggested is not prescriptive and the teacher will, of course, feel free to select and rearrange the material to suit the needs of particular students and classes.

Ray Speakman

List of Characters

Delegates of the Calinsk goat-breeding
  kolchos: an old peasant, a peasant woman, a
  young peasant, a very young workman.
Members of the Rosa Luxemburg
  fruit-growing kolchos: an old peasant, a
  peasant woman, the agronomist, the girl
  tractor driver; the wounded soldier and
  other peasants from the kolchos.
The expert from the capital.
The singer Arkadi Cheidze.
His musicians.
Georgi Abashvili, the Governor.
His wife, Natella.
Their son, Michael.
Shalva, the adjutant.
Arsen Kazbeki, the fat prince.
The rider from the capital.
Niko Mikadze and Mikha Loladze, doctors.
Simon Chachava, a soldier.
Grusha Vachnadze, a kitchen-maid.
Three architects.
Four chambermaids: Assia, Masha, Sulika and
  Fat Nina.
A nurse.
A man cook.
A woman cook.
A stableman.
Servants in the Governor's palace.
The Governor's and the fat prince's Ironshirts
  and soldiers.

Beggars and petitioners.
The old peasant with the milk.
Two elegant ladies.
The innkeeper.
The servant.
A corporal.
'Blockhead', a soldier.
A peasant woman and her husband.
Three merchants.
Lavrenti Vachnadze, Grusha's brother.
His wife, Aniko.
Their stableman.
The peasant woman, for a time Grusha's
  mother-in-law.
Yussup, her son.
Brother Anastasius, a monk.
Wedding guests.
Children.
Azdak, the village clerk.
Shauva, a policeman.
A refugee, the Grand Duke.
The doctor.
The invalid.
The limping man.
The blackmailer.
Ludovica, the innkeeper's daughter-in-law.
A poor old peasant woman.
Her brother-in-law Irakli, a bandit.
Three farmers.
Illo Shaboladze and Sandro Oboladze, lawyers.
The very old married couple.

Collaborator: R. BERLAU
Translators: JAMES AND TANIA STERN, *with* W.H. AUDEN

The Caucasian Chalk Circle

1

The Struggle for the Valley

Among the ruins of a badly shelled Caucasian village the members of two kolchos villages are sitting in a circle, smoking and drinking wine. They consist mainly of women and old men, but there are also a few soldiers among them. With them is an expert of the State Reconstruction Commission from the capital.

A PEASANT WOMAN *(left, pointing)* In those hills over there we stopped three Nazi tanks. But the apple orchard had already been destroyed.

‘ AN OLD PEASANT *(right)* Our beautiful dairy farm. All in ruins.

A GIRL TRACTOR DRIVER *(left)* I set fire to it, Comrade.

Pause.

THE EXPERT Now listen to the report: the delegates of the Galinsk goat-breeding kolchos arrived in Nukha. When the Hitler armies were approaching, the kolchos had been ordered by the authorities to move its goat-herds further to the east. The kolchos now considers resettling in this valley. Its delegates have investigated the village and the grounds and found a high degree of destruction. (*The delegates on the right nod.*) The neighbouring Rosa Luxemburg fruit-growing kolchos (*to the left*) moves that the former grazing land of the Galinsk kolchos, a valley with scanty growth of grass, should be used for the replanting of orchards and vineyards. As an expert of the Reconstruction Commission, I request the two kolchos villages to decide between themselves whether the Galinsk kolchos shall return here or not.

AN OLD MAN *(right)* First of all, I want to protest against the restriction of time for discussion. We of the Galinsk kolchos have spent three days and three nights getting here. And now we are allowed a discussion of only half a day.

A WOUNDED SOLDIER *(left)* Comrade, we no longer have as many villages and no longer as many working hands and no longer as much time.

THE GIRL TRACTOR DRIVER	(*left*) All pleasures have to be rationed. Tobacco is rationed, and wine and discussion, too.
THE OLD MAN	(*right, sighing*) Death to the Fascists! But I will come to the point and explain to you why we want to have our valley back. There are a great many reasons, but I want to begin with one of the simplest. Makinae Abakidze, unpack the goat cheese.

A peasant woman, right, takes from a basket an enor- mous cheese wrapped in a cloth. Applause and laughter.

	Help yourselves, comrades. Start in.
AN OLD PEASANT	(*left, suspiciously*) Is this meant to influence us, perhaps?
THE OLD MAN	(*right, amidst laughter*) How could it be meant as an influence, Surab, you valley-thief? Everyone knows that you will take the cheese and the valley, too. (*Laughter*) All I expect from you is an honest answer: Do you like the cheese?
THE OLD MAN	(*left*) The answer is yes.
THE OLD MAN	(*right*) Oh. (*Bitterly*) I might have guessed you know nothing about cheese.
THE OLD MAN	(*left*) Why not? When I tell you I like it!
THE OLD MAN	(*right*) Because you can't like it. Because it's not what it was in the old days. And why isn't it? Because our goats don't like the new grass as they used to like the old. Cheese is not cheese because grass is not grass, that's it. Mind you put that in your report.
THE OLD MAN	(*left*) But your cheese is excellent.
THE OLD MAN	(*right*) It's not excellent. Barely decent. The new grazing land is no good, whatever the young people may say. I tell you, it's impossible to live there. It doesn't even smell of morning there in the morning.

Several people laugh.

THE EXPERT	Don't mind their laughter. They understand you all the same. Comrades, why does one love one's country? Because the bread tastes better there, the sky is higher, the air smells better, voices sound stronger, the ground is easier to walk on. Isn't that so?

THE OLD MAN	(*right*) The valley has belonged to us for centuries.
THE SOLDIER	(*left*) What does that mean – for centuries? Nothing belongs to anyone for centuries. When you were young you didn't even belong to yourself, but to Prince Kazbeki.
THE OLD MAN	(*right*) According to the law the valley belongs to us.
THE GIRL TRACTOR DRIVER	The laws will have to be re-examined in any case, to see whether they are still valid.
THE OLD MAN	(*right*) That's obvious. You mean to say it makes no difference what kind of tree stands beside the house where one was born? Or what kind of neighbour one has? Doesn't that make any difference? We want to go back just to have you next door to our kolchos, you valley-thieves. Now you can laugh that one off.
THE OLD MAN	(*left, laughing*) Then why don't you listen to what your 'neighbour', Kato Vachtang, our agronomist, has to say about the valley?
A PEASANT WOMAN	(*right*) We haven't said anywhere near all we have to say about our valley. Not all the houses are destroyed. At least the foundation wall of the dairy farm is still standing.
THE EXPERT	You can claim State support – both here and there. You know that.
A PEASANT WOMAN	(*right*) Comrade Expert, we're not trading now. I can't take your cap and hand you another, and say: 'This one's better.' The other one might be better, but you prefer yours.
THE GIRL TRACTOR DRIVER	A piece of land is not like a cap. Not in our country, comrade.
THE EXPERT	Don't get angry. It's true that we have to consider a piece of land as a tool with which one produces something useful. But it's also true that we must recognize the love for a particular piece of land. Before we continue the discussion I suggest that you explain to the comrades

of the Galinsk kolchos just what you intend to do with the disputed valley.

THE OLD MAN (*right*) Agreed.

THE OLD MAN (*left*) Yes, let Kato speak.

THE EXPERT Comrade Agronomist!

THE AGRONOMIST (*rising. She is in military uniform.*) Last winter, comrades, while we were fighting here in these hills as partisans, we discussed how after the expulsion of the Germans we could increase our orchards to ten times their former size. I have prepared a plan for an irrigation project. With the help of a dam on our mountain lake, three hundred hectares of unfertile land can be irrigated. Our kolchos could then grow not only more fruit, but wine as well. The project, however, would pay only if the disputed valley of the Galinsk kolchos could also be included. Here are the calculations. (*She hands* THE EXPERT *a briefcase.*)

THE OLD MAN (*right*) Write into the report that our kolchos plans to start a new stud farm.

THE GIRL TRACTOR DRIVER Comrades, the project was conceived during the days and nights when we had to take cover in the mountains and often were without ammunition for our few rifles. Even to get a pencil was difficult.

Applause from both sides.

THE OLD MAN (*right*) Our thanks to the comrades of the Rosa Luxemburg kolchos and to all those who defended our country.

They shake hands and embrace.

THE PEASANT WOMAN (*left*) Our thoughts were that our soldiers – both your men and our men – should return to a still more fertile homeland.

THE GIRL TRACTOR DRIVER As the poet Mayakovsky said: 'The home of the Soviet people shall also be the home of Reason!'

The delegates on the right (except THE OLD MAN*) have risen and, with* THE EXPERT, *study* THE AGRONOMIST'S *plans. Exclamations such as: 'Why is there a fall of 66 feet?' – 'This rock here is to be dynamited' – 'Actually, all they need is cement and dynamite!' – 'They force the water to come down here, that's clever!'*

A VERY YOUNG WORKMAN	(*right, to* THE OLD MAN, *right*) They are going to irrigate all the fields between the hills – look at that, Alleko.
THE OLD MAN	(*right*) I am not going to look at it. I knew the project would be good. I won't have a revolver pointed at my chest.
THE SOLDIER	But they are only pointing a pencil at your chest.

Laughter

THE OLD MAN	(*right. He gets up gloomily and walks over to look at the drawings.*) These valley-thieves know only too well that we can't resist machines and projects in this country.
THE PEASANT WOMAN	(*right*) Alleko Bereshvili, you yourself are the worst one at new projects. That is well known.
THE EXPERT	What about my report? May I write that in your kolchos you will support the transfer of your old valley for the project?
THE PEASANT WOMAN	(*right*) I will support it. What about you, Alleko?
THE OLD MAN	(*right, bent over the drawings*) I move that you give us copies of the drawings to take along.
THE PEASANT WOMAN	(*right*) Then we can sit down to eat. Once he has the drawings and is ready to discuss them, the affair is settled. I know him. And it will be the same with the rest of us.

The delegates embrace again amidst laughter.

THE OLD MAN	(*left*) Long live the Galinsk kolchos and good luck to your new stud farm!
THE PEASANT WOMAN	(*left*) Comrades, in honour of the visit of the delegates from the Galinsk kolchos and of the expert we have arranged a play featuring the singer Arkadi Cheidze, which has some bearing on our problem.

Applause.

THE GIRL TRACTOR *driver has gone off to fetch* THE SINGER.

THE PEASANT WOMAN	(*right*) Comrades, your play will have to be good. We're going to pay for it with a valley.
THE PEASANT WOMAN	(*left*) Arkadi Cheidze knows 21,000 verses by heart.

THE OLD MAN   (*left*) We rehearsed the play under his direction. It is very difficult to get him, by the way. You and the Planning Commission should see to it that he comes north more often, comrade.

THE EXPERT   We are more concerned with economy.

THE OLD MAN   (*left, smiling*) You arrange the new distribution of grapevines and tractors. Why not of songs, too?

Enter the singer ARKADI CHEIDZE, *led by* THE GIRL TRACTOR DRIVER. *He is a sturdy man of simple manners, accompanied by musicians with their instruments. The artists are greeted with applause.*

THE GIRL TRACTOR DRIVER   This is the comrade expert, Arkadi.

THE SINGER *greets those round him.*

THE PEASANT WOMAN   (*right*) I am very honoured to make your acquaintance. I've heard about your songs ever since I was at school.

THE SINGER   This time it's a play with songs, and almost the whole kolchos takes part. We have brought along the old masks.

THE OLD MAN   (*right*) Is it going to be one of the old legends?

THE SINGER   A very old one. It is called 'The Chalk Circle' and is derived from the Chinese. But we will recite it in a changed version. Yura, show the masks. Comrades, we consider it an honour to entertain you after such a difficult debate. We hope you will find that the voice of the old poet also sounds well in the shadow of Soviet tractors. It may be mistaken to mix different wines, but old and new wisdom mix very well. Now I hope we will all be given something to eat before the recital begins. That usually helps.

VOICES   Of course. – Everyone into the club house.

All go cheerfully to the meal. While they begin to move off, THE EXPERT *turns to the singer.*

THE EXPERT   How long will the story take, Arkadi? I have to get back to Tiflis tonight.

THE SINGER   (*casually*) It is actually two stories. A few hours.

THE EXPERT   (*very confidentially*) Couldn't you make it shorter?

THE SINGER   No.

2

The Noble Child

THE SINGER *who is seen sitting on the floor in front of his musicians, a black sheepskin cloak round his shoulders, leafing through a small, well-thumbed script:*

Once upon a time
A time of bloodshed
When this city was called
The city of the damned
It had a Governor.
His name was Georgi Abashvili
Once upon a time.

He was very rich
He had a beautiful wife
He had a healthy child
Once upon a time.

No other governor in Grusinia
Had as many horses in his stable
As many beggars on his doorstep
As many soldiers in his service
As many petitioners in his courtyard
Once upon a time.

Georgi Abashvili, how shall I describe him?
He enjoyed his life:
On Easter Sunday morning
The Governor and his family went to church
Once upon a time.

Beggars and petitioners stream from a palace gateway, holding up thin children, crutches, and petitions. They are followed by two Ironshirts and then by the Governor's family, elaborately dressed.

THE BEGGARS AND PETITIONERS Mercy, Your Grace, the taxes are
beyond our means ... I lost my leg in the

Persian War, where can I get … My brother is
innocent, Your Grace, a misunderstanding … My
child is starving in my arms … We plead for our son's
discharge from the army, our one remaining son …
Please, Your Grace, the water inspector is corrupt.

*A servant collects the petitions, another distributes
coins from a purse. Soldiers push back the crowd,
lashing at it with thick leather whips.*

SOLDIER   Get back! Make way at the church door!

Behind the GOVERNOR, *his* WIFE *and his* ADJUTANT, *the
Governor's child is driven through the gateway in
an ornate pram. The crowd surges forward to see it.*

THE SINGER   *while the crowd is driven back with whips:*

> For the first time on this Easter Sunday,
>   the people see the heir.
> Two doctors never leave the child, the noble child
> Apple of the Governor's eye.

*Cries from the crowd: 'The child' 'I can't see it, stop
pushing!' … 'God bless the child, Your Grace!'*

THE SINGER   Even the mighty Prince Kazbeki
Bows before it at the church door.

A FAT PRINCE *steps forward and bows before the family.*

THE FAT PRINCE   Happy Easter, Natella Abashvili!

*A command is heard. A rider arrives at the gallop
and holds out to* THE GOVERNOR *a roll of documents.
At a nod from* THE GOVERNOR, THE ADJUTANT, *a
handsome young man, approaches the rider and
stops him. There follows a brief pause during which*
THE FAT PRINCE *eyes the rider suspiciously.*

THE FAT PRINCE   What a magnificent day! While it was raining in the
night I thought to myself: gloomy holidays. But this
morning: a gay sky. I love a bright sky, a simple heart,
Natella Abashvili. And little Michael, a governor from
head to foot, tititi! (*He tickles the child.*) Happy
Easter, little Michael, tititi!

THE GOVERNOR'S
WIFE   What do you think of this, Arsen? Georgi
has finally decided to start building the new

wing on the east side. All these miserable slum houses are to be torn down to make room for a garden.

THE FAT PRINCE That's good news after so much bad. What's the latest about the war, Brother Georgi? (THE GOVERNOR *shows his lack of interest.*) A strategic retreat, I hear? Well, minor reverses invariably occur. Sometimes things go well, sometimes not so well. Such are the fortunes of war. Doesn't mean much, eh?

THE GOVERNOR'S WIFE He's coughing! Georgi, did you hear?

Sharply to the two doctors, dignified men, who stand close to the pram He's coughing!

FIRST DOCTOR (*to the second*) May I remind you, Niko Mikadze, that I was against the lukewarm bath? A minor oversight in warming the bath water, Your Grace.

SECOND DOCTOR (*equally polite*) I can't possibly agree with you, Mikha Loladze. The temperature of the bath water was the one prescribed by our great and beloved Mishiko Oboladze. More likely a slight draught in the night, Your Grace.

THE GOVERNOR'S WIFE But do take better care of him. He looks feverish, Georgi.

FIRST DOCTOR (*bending over the child*) No cause for alarm, Your Grace. The bath water will be warmer. It won't happen again.

SECOND DOCTOR (*with a poisonous glance at the first*) I won't forget it, dear Mikha Loladze. No cause for alarm, Your Grace.

THE FAT PRINCE Well, well, well! I always say: one pain in my liver and the doctor gets fifty strokes on the soles of his feet. And that's only because we live in such a decadent age. In the old days it would have been: Off with his head!

THE GOVERNOR'S WIFE Let's go into the church. Very likely it's the draught here.

The procession, consisting of the family and servants, turns into the church doorway. THE FAT PRINCE *follows.* THE ADJUTANT *leaves the procession and points at the rider.*

THE GOVERNOR	Not before divine service, Shalva.
ADJUTANT	(*to the rider*) The Governor doesn't want to be bothered with reports before the service – especially if they are, as I suspect, of a depressing nature. Go and get yourself something to eat in the kitchen, my friend.

THE ADJUTANT *joins the procession while the rider enters the palace gateway, cursing. A soldier appears from the palace and remains standing in the gateway.*

THE SINGER	The city lies still. On the church square the pigeons preen themselves. A soldier of the palace guard Is jesting with the kitchen maid As she comes up from the river with a bundle.

A girl tries to pass through the gateway, a bundle of large green leaves under her arm.

THE SOLDIER	What! The young lady is not in church? Shirking service?
GRUSHA	I was already dressed to go. But they wanted one more goose for the Easter banquet. And they asked me to fetch it. I know something about geese.
THE SOLDIER	A goose? (*Feigning suspicion.*) I'd like to see that goose. GRUSHA *doesn't understand.* One has to be on one's guard with women. They say: 'I only went to fetch a goose', and then it turns out to be something quite different.
GRUSHA	(*walks resolutely towards him and shows him the goose*) There it is. And if it isn't a fifteen-pound goose, and they haven't stuffed it with corn, I'll eat the feathers.
THE SOLDIER	A queen of a goose. It will be eaten by the Governor himself. So the young lady has been down to the river again?
GRUSHA	Yes, at the poultry farm.
THE SOLDIER	I see! At the poultry farm, down by the river. Not higher up, near those – those willows?
GRUSHA	I go to the willows only to wash linen.

THE SOLDIER	(*insinuatingly*) Exactly.
GRUSHA	Exactly what?
THE SOLDIER	(*winking*) Exactly that.
GRUSHA	Why shouldn't I wash my linen near the willows?
THE SOLDIER	(*with exaggerated laughter*) 'Why shouldn't I wash my linen near the willows!' That's a good one, that is!
GRUSHA	I don't understand the soldier. What's so good about it?
THE SOLDIER	(*slyly*) If someone knew what someone's told, she'd grow hot, she'd grow cold.
GRUSHA	I don't know what I could know about those willows.
THE SOLDIER	Not even if there were a bush opposite? From which everything could be seen? Everything that happens there when a certain person is washing linen?
GRUSHA	What happens there? Won't the soldier say what he means and have done with it?
THE SOLDIER	Something happens. And perhaps something can be seen.
GRUSHA	Could the soldier mean that – once in a while on a hot day – I put my toes in the water? For otherwise there's nothing.
THE SOLDIER	And more – the toes and more.
GRUSHA	More what? At most the foot.
THE SOLDIER	The foot and a little more. (*He laughs heartily.*)
GRUSHA	(*angrily*) Simon Chachava, you ought to be ashamed of yourself! To sit in a bush on a hot day and wait till someone comes along and puts her leg in the river! And most likely with another soldier! (*She runs off.*)
THE SOLDIER	(*shouting after her*) Not with another soldier!
	As the singer resumes his story THE SOLDIER *runs after* GRUSHA.
THE SINGER	The city lies still, but why are there armed men? The Governor's palace lies at peace But why is it a fortress?

From the doorway at the left THE FAT PRINCE *enters quickly. He stands still and looks around. Before the gateway at the right two Ironshirts are waiting. Noticing them, the prince walks slowly past them, signs to them, then exits quickly. One Ironshirt exits through the gateway, the other remains on guard. Muffled voices come from different sides in the rear: 'To your posts!' The palace is surrounded. Distant church bells. Enter through the doorway the procession and the Governor's family returning from church.*

THE SINGER   Then the Governor returned to his palace
Then the fortress was a trap
Then the goose was plucked and roasted
Then the goose was no longer eaten
Then noon was no longer the hour to eat
Then noon was the hour to die.

THE GOVERNOR'S WIFE   (*in passing*) It's quite impossible to live in this slum. But Georgi, of course, builds only for his little Michael! Never for me. Michael is everything, everything for Michael!

THE GOVERNOR   Did you hear Brother Kazbeki bid me a 'Happy Easter'? That's all very well, but so far as I know it didn't rain in Nukha last night. It rained where Brother Kazbeki was. Where was Brother Kazbeki?

THE ADJUTANT   That will have to be investigated.

THE GOVERNOR   Yes, at once. Tomorrow.

The procession turns into the gateway. The rider, who has meanwhile returned from the palace, walks towards THE GOVERNOR.

THE ADJUTANT   Don't you want to listen to the rider from the capital, Your Excellency? He arrived this morning with confidential papers.

THE GOVERNOR   (*in passing*) Not before the banquet, Shalva!

THE ADJUTANT   (*to the rider, while the procession disappears into the palace and only two Ironshirts remain at the gate as palace guards*) The Governor doesn't wish to be disturbed by military reports before the banquet. The afternoon His Excellency will devote to conferences with prominent architects who have also been invited to the banquet. Here they are already. (*Enter three men. As the rider goes off,* THE ADJUTANT *greets the architects.*) Gentlemen, His Excellency is awaiting you at the banquet. His entire time will be devoted to you. To the great new plans! Come, let us go!

ONE OF THE ARCHITECTS   We are impressed that his Excellency thinks of building in spite of the disquieting rumours that the war in Persia has taken a turn for the worse.

THE ADJUTANT   All the more reason for building! That's nothing. Persia is far away. The garrison here would let itself be chopped to pieces for its Governor.
Uproar from the palace. Shrill screams of a woman. Orders are shouted. Dumbfounded, THE ADJUTANT *moves towards the gateway. An Ironshirt steps out and holds him up at the point of a lance.*
What's going on here? Put down that lance, you dog! (*To the palace guard, furiously*) Disarm him! Can't you see an attempt is being made on the Governor's life?

The palace guard Ironshirts refuse to obey. Staring coldly, indifferently, at THE ADJUTANT, *they watch the proceedings without interest.* THE ADJUTANT *fights his way into the palace.*

ONE OF THE ARCHITECTS   The Princes! Don't you realize that the Princes met last night in the capital? And that they are against the Grand Duke and his governors? Gentlemen, we'd better make ourselves scarce.

They rush off.

THE SINGER   Oh, blindness of the great! They walk like gods
Great over bent backs, sure
Of hired fists, trusting
In their power which has already lasted so long.
But long is not forever.
Oh, Wheel of Fortune! Hope of the people!

From the gateway, enter THE GOVERNOR *with a grey face, manacled, between two soldiers armed to the teeth.*

Walk, Your Highness, walk even now with head up.
From your Palace the eyes of many foes follow you!
You no longer need an architect, a carpenter will do.

You will not move into a new palace, but into a little
hole in the ground.
Just look about you once more, you blind man!
The arrested GOVERNOR *looks about him.*
Does all you once possessed still please you?
Between the Easter Mass and the banquet.
You are walking to that place from which no one
returns.
THE GOVERNOR *is led away. The palace guard
follows. A horn sounds. Noise behind the gateway.*
When the houses of the great collapse
Many little people are slain.
Those who had no share in the fortunes of the mighty
Often have a share in their misfortunes. The plunging
wain
Drags the sweating beasts with it into the abyss.
Servants come rushing through the gateway in panic.

THE SERVANTS	(*in confusion*) The hampers! – Take them all into the third courtyard! Food for five days! – Her Ladyship has fainted! Someone must carry her down. She must get away. – And what about us? We'll be slaughtered like chickens, it's the old story. – Jesus and Mary, what's going to happen? There's already bloodshed in the town, they say. – Nonsense, the Governor has just been asked politely to appear at a Princes' meeting. Everything'll be all right. I have this on the best authority.

The two doctors rush into the courtyard.

FIRST DOCTOR	(*trying to restrain the other*) Niko Mikadze, it is your duty as a doctor to attend Natella Abashvili.
SECOND DOCTOR	My duty? It's yours!
FIRST DOCTOR	Niko Mikadze, who is in charge of the child today? You or me?
SECOND DOCTOR	Do you really think, Mikha Loladze, I'm going to stay another minute in this cursed house for that little brat?

*They start fighting. All one hears is: 'You neglect
your duty!' and 'Duty be damned!' Then the second
doctor knocks down the first.*

SECOND DOCTOR	Oh, go to hell! (*Exit.*)

THE SERVANTS	There's time enough before night. The soldiers won't be drunk till then. – Does anyone know if they've started a mutiny yet? – The Palace Guard has ridden away. – Doesn't anyone know what's happened?
GRUSHA	Meliva the fisherman says a comet with a red tail has been seen in the sky over the capital. That means bad luck.
THE SERVANTS	Yesterday they were saying in the capital that the Persian War is lost. – The Princes have started a great revolt. There's a rumour that the Grand Duke has already fled. All his Governors are to be hanged. – The likes of us will be left alone. I have a brother in the Ironshirts.

Enter the soldier SIMON CHACHAVA, *searching the crowd for* GRUSHA.

THE ADJUTANT	(*appearing in the doorway*) Everyone into the third courtyard! All hands help with the packing!

He drives the servants out. SIMON *finally finds* GRUSHA.

SIMON	There you are at last, Grusha! What are you going to do?
GRUSHA	Nothing. If the worst comes to the worst, I've a brother with a farm in the mountains. But what about you?
SIMON	Don't worry about me. (*Polite again*) Grusha Vachnadze, your desire to know my plans fills me with satisfaction. I've been ordered to accompany Madam Natella Abashvili as her guard.
GRUSHA	But hasn't the Palace Guard mutinied?
SIMON	(*serious*) That they have.
GRUSHA	But isn't it dangerous to accompany the woman?
SIMON	In Tiflis they say: how can stabbing harm the knife?
GRUSHA	You're not a knife. You're a man, Simon Chachava. What has this woman to do with you?
SIMON	The woman has nothing to do with me. But I have my orders, and so I go.
GRUSHA	The soldier is a pig-headed man; he gets himself into danger for nothing – nothing at all. (*As she is called from the palace*) Now I must go into the third courtyard. I'm in a hurry.

SIMON   As there's a hurry we oughtn't to quarrel. For a good quarrel one needs time. May I ask if the young lady still has parents?

GRUSHA   No, only a brother.

SIMON   As time is short – the second question would be: Is the young lady as healthy as a fish in water?

GRUSHA   Perhaps once in a while a pain in the right shoulder; but otherwise strong enough for any work. So far no one has complained.

SIMON   Everyone knows that. Even if it's Easter Sunday and there's the question who shall fetch the goose, then it's she. The third question is this: Is the young lady impatient? Does she want cherries in winter?

GRUSHA   Impatient, no. But if a man goes to war without any reason, and no message comes, that's bad.

SIMON   A message will come. (GRUSHA *is again called from the palace.*) And finally the main question ...

GRUSHA   Simon Chachava, because I've got to go to the third courtyard and I'm in a hurry, the answer is 'Yes'.

SIMON   (*very embarrassed*)Hurry, they say, is the wind that blows down the scaffolding. But they also say: The rich don't know what hurry is. – I come from ...

GRUSHA   Kurtsk.

SIMON   So the young lady has already made inquiries? Am healthy, have no dependants, earn ten piastres a month, as a paymaster twenty, and am asking honourably for your hand.

GRUSHA   Simon Chachava, that suits me.

SIMON   (*taking from his neck a thin chain from which hangs a little cross*) This cross belonged to my mother, Grusha Vachnadze. The chain is silver. Please wear it.

GRUSHA   I thank you, Simon. (*He fastens it round her neck.*)

SIMON   Now I must harness the horses. The young lady will understand that. It would be better for the young lady to go into the third courtyard. Otherwise there'll be trouble.

GRUSHA   Yes, Simon.

They stand together undecided.

SIMON I'll just take the woman to the troops who've remained loyal. When the war's over, I'll come back. In two weeks. Or three. I hope my intended won't get tired waiting for my return.

GRUSHA Simon Chachava, I shall wait for you.

> Go calmly into battle, soldier
> The bloody battle, the bitter battle
> From which not everyone returns.
> When you return I will be there.
> I will be waiting for you under the green elm
> I will be waiting for you under the bare elm
> I will wait until the last soldier has returned
> And even longer.
> When you return from the battle
> No boots will lie before the door
> The pillow beside mine will be empty
> My mouth will be unkissed.
> When you return, when you return
> You will be able to say: all is as it was.

SIMON I thank you, Grusha Vachnadze, and farewell!
He bows low before her; she bows low before him. Then she runs off without looking round. Enter THE ADJUTANT *from the gateway.*

THE ADJUTANT (*harshly*) Harness the horses to the big carriage! Don't stand there doing nothing, idiot!
SIMON CHACHAVA *leaps to attention and goes off. Two servants crawl in from the gateway, loaded down with heavy truncks. Behind them, supported by her women, stumbles* NATELLA ABASHVILL *She is followed by another woman carrying Michael.*

THE GOVERNOR'S WIFE As usual, nobody's paying the slightest attention. I hardly know if I'm standing on my head or my feet. Where's Michael? Don't hold him so clumsily! Pile the trunks on to the carriage! Shalva, is there any word from the Governor?

THE ADJUTANT (*shaking his head*) You must get away at once.

THE GOVERNOR'S WIFE Is there any news from the town?

THE ADJUTANT	No. So far all is quiet. But there isn't a minute to lose. There's not enough room for the trunks on the carriage. Please pick out what you need.

Exit THE ADJUTANT *quickly.*

THE GOVERNOR'S WIFE	Only essentials! Quick, open the trunks. I'll tell you what I've got to have.

The trunks are lowered and opened.

THE GOVERNOR'S WIFE	(*pointing at some brocade dresses*) That green one! And of course that one with the fur trimming. Where are the doctors? I'm getting this terrible migraine again. It always starts in the temples. This one with the little pearl buttons … (*Enter* GRUSHA.) You're taking your time, eh? Go and get the hot water bottles at once!

GRUSHA *runs off, and returns with hot water bottles.* THE GOVERNOR'S WIFE *orders her about by signs.*

THE GOVERNOR'S WIFE	(*watching a young woman attendant*) Don't tear the sleeve!
THE YOUNG WOMAN	I promise you, madam, no harm has come to the dress.
THE GOVERNOR'S WIFE	Because I caught you. I've been watching you for a long time. Nothing in your head but making eyes at the Adjutant. I'll kill you, you bitch! (*She beats her.*)
THE ADJUTANT	(*returning*) I must ask you to make haste, Natella Abashvili. They are fighting in the town. *Exit* THE ADJUTANT.
THE GOVERNOR'S WIFE	(*letting go of* THE YOUNG WOMAN) My God, do you think they'll do something to me? Why should they? (*All are silent. She herself begins to rummage in the trunks.*) Where's my brocade jacket? Help me! What about Michael? Is he asleep?
THE NURSE	Yes, madam.
THE GOVERNOR'S WIFE	Then put him down a moment and go and fetch my little morocco slippers from the bedchamber. I need them to go with the green dress. (THE NURSE *puts down the child and goes off. To the young woman*) Don't

stand around, you! (THE YOUNG WOMAN *runs off.*) Stay here, or I'll have you flogged! Just look at the way these things have been packed! No love! No understanding! If one doesn't give every order oneself ... At such moments one realizes what one's servants are like! Masha! (*She gives her an order with a wave of the hand.*) You all gorge yourselves, but never a sign of gratitude! I won't forget this.

THE ADJUTANT (*very excited*) Natella, you must leave at once! Orbeliani, Judge of the Supreme Court, has just been hanged! The carpet weavers are in revolt!

THE GOVERNOR'S WIFE Why? I must have the silver dress – it cost 1000 piastres. And that one there, and all my furs. And where's the wine-coloured dress?

THE ADJUTANT (*trying to pull her away*) Riots have broken out in the outer town! We've got to leave this minute! (*A servant runs off.*) Where's the child?

THE GOVERNOR'S WIFE (*to* THE NURSE) Maro, get the child ready! Where are you?

THE ADJUTANT (*leaving*) We'll probably have to do without the carriage. And ride.

THE GOVERNOR'S WIFE *still rummages among her dresses, throws some on the heap to go with her, then takes them off again. Drums are heard. The sky begins to redden.*

THE GOVERNOR'S WIFE (*rummaging desperately*) I can't find that wine-coloured dress. (*Shrugging her shoulders, to the second woman*) Take the whole heap and carry it to the carriage. Why hasn't Maro come back? Have you all gone off your heads? I told you it's right at the bottom.

THE ADJUTANT (*returning*) Quick! Quick!

THE GOVERNOR'S WIFE (*to the second woman*) Run! Just throw them into the carriage!

THE ADJUTANT We're not going by carriage. Come at once or I'll ride off on my own!

THE GOVERNOR'S WIFE Maro! Bring the child! (*To the second woman*) Go and look, Masha. No, first take the dresses to the carriage. It's all nonsense, I wouldn't dream of riding! (*Turning round, she sees the fire-reddened sky and starts back in horror.*) Fire! (*She rushes off, followed by* THE ADJUTANT. *The second woman, shaking her head, follows with a heap of dresses. Servants enter from the gateway.*)

THE COOK   That must be the East Gate that's burning.

THE CHEF   They've gone. And without the food wagon. How are we going to get away now?

A STABLEMAN   This is going to be an unhealthy place for some time. (*To the third chambermaid*) Suleika, I'm going to fetch some blankets, we're clearing out.

THE NURSE   (*entering through the gateway with her mistress's slippers*) Madam!

A FAT WOMAN   She's gone.

THE NURSE   And the child! (*She rushes to the child, and picks it up.*) They left it behind, those brutes! (*She hands the child to* GRUSHA.) Hold it for a moment. (*Deceitfully*) I'm going to look for the carriage.

              She runs off, following THE GOVERNOR'S WIFE.

GRUSHA   What have they done to the Governor?

THE STABLEMAN (*drawing his index finger across his throat*) Fft.

THE FAT WOMAN (*seeing the gesture, becomes hysterical*) Oh God! Oh God! Oh God! Our master Georgi Abashvili! At morning Mass he was a picture of health! And now! Oh, take me away! We're all lost! We must die in sin! Like our master, Georgi Abashvili!

THE THIRD WOMAN (*trying to calm her*) Calm down, Nina. You'll get away. You've done no one any harm.

THE FAT WOMAN (*being led out*) Oh God! Oh God! Oh God! Let's all get out before they come! Before they come!

THE THIRD WOMAN Nina takes it to heart more than the mistress. People like that get others even to do their weeping for them! (*Seeing the child in* GRUSHA'*s arms*) The child! What are you doing with it?

GRUSHA   It's been left behind.

THE THIRD WOMAN She just left it? Michael, who was never allowed to be in a draught!

              The servants gather round the child.

GRUSHA   He's waking up.

THE STABLEMAN	Better put him down, I tell you. I'd rather not think what'd happen to the person seen with that child. I'll get our things. You wait here. (*Exit into the palace.*)
THE COOK	He's right. Once they start they slaughter whole families. I'll go and fetch my belongings.

All go except THE COOK, THE THIRD WOMAN *and* GRUSHA *with the child in her arms.*

THE THIRD WOMAN	Didn't you hear? Better put him down!
GRUSHA	The nurse asked me to hold him for a moment.
THE COOK	That one won't come back, you silly!
THE THIRD WOMAN	Keep your hands off him.
THE COOK	They'll be more after him than after his mother. He's the heir. Grusha, you're a good soul. But you know you're not too bright. I tell you, if he had the plague it couldn't be worse. Better see to it that you get away.

THE STABLEMAN *has come back carrying bundles which he distributes among the women. All except* GRUSHA *prepare to leave.*

GRUSHA	(*stubbornly*) He hasn't got the plague. He looks at you like a human being.
THE COOK	Then don't you look back. You're just the kind of fool who always gets put upon. If someone says to you: Run and get the lettuce, you have the longest legs! – you run. We're taking the ox-cart, you can have a lift if you hurry. Jesus, by now the whole neighbourhood must be in flames!
THE THIRD WOMAN	Haven't you packed anything yet? There isn't much time, you know. The Ironshirts will soon be here from the barracks.

Exit both women and THE STABLEMAN.

GRUSHA	I'm coming.

GRUSHA *lays the child down, looks at it for a moment, then takes clothes from the trunks lying about and covers the sleeping child. Then she runs into the palace to get her things. Sounds of horses' hoofs and of women screaming. Enter* THE FAT PRINCE *with drunken Ironshirts. One of them carries the head of* THE GOVERNOR *on a lance.*

THE FAT PRINCE	Put it here. Right in the middle! (*One Ironshirt climbs on to the back of another, takes the head and holds it*

over the gateway.) That's not the middle. Further to the right. Good. What I do, my friends, I do well. (*While an Ironshirt with hammer and nail fastens the head by its hair.*) This morning at the church door I said to Georgi Abashvili: 'I love a clear sky'. Actually, what I prefer is lightning from a clear sky. Oh, yes. But it's a pity they took the brat away. I need him. Badly. Search the whole of Grusinia for him! 1000 piastres reward!

As GRUSHA *enters cautiously through the doorway,* THE FAT PRINCE *and the Ironshirts leave. Trampling of horses' hoofs again. Carrying a bundle,* GRUSHA *walks towards the gateway. At the last moment, she turns to see if the child is still there. Promptly* THE SINGER *begins to sing. She stands rooted to the spot.*

THE SINGER   As she was standing between courtyard and gate, she heard
Or thought she heard, a low voice. The child
Called to her, not whining but calling quite sensibly
At least so it seemed to her: 'Woman', it said, 'Help me'.
Went on calling not whining but calling quite sensibly:
'Don't you know, woman, that she who does not listen to a cry for help
But passes by shutting her ears, will never hear
The gentle call of a lover
Nor the blackbird at dawn, nor the happy
Sigh of the exhausted grape-picker at the sound of the Angelus.'
Hearing this

GRUSHA *walks a few steps towards the child and bends over it.*
                        she went back to the child
Just for one more look, just to sit with it
For a moment or two till someone should come
Its mother, perhaps, or someone else –

She sits down opposite the child, and leans against a trunk.
Just for a moment before she left, for now the danger was too great
The city full of flame and grief.

The light grows dimmer as though evening and night were falling, GRUSHA *has gone into the palace and fetched a lamp and some milk, which she gives the child to drink.*

THE SINGER (*loudly*)

Terrible is the temptation to do good!

GRUSHA *now settles down to keep watch over the child through the night. Once, she lights a small lamp to look at it. Once, she tucks it in with a brocade coat. Now and again she listens and looks up to see if someone is coming.*

For a long time she sat with the child.
Evening came, night came, dawn came.
Too long she sat, too long she watched
The soft breathing, the little fists
Till towards morning the temptation grew too
    strong.
She rose, she leaned over, she sighed, she lifted the
    child
She carried it off.

She does what the singer says as he describes it.
Like booty she took it for herself
Like a thief she sneaked away.

3
The Flight into the Northern Mountains

THE SINGER

As Grusha Vachnadze left the city
On the Grusinian Highway
Towards the northern mountains
She sang a song, she bought some milk.

THE MUSICIANS

How will the merciful escape the merciless
The bloodhounds, the trappers?
Into the deserted mountains she wandered
Along the Grusinian highway she wandered
She sang a song, she bought some milk.

GRUSHA VACHNADZE *continues on her way. On her back she carries the child in a sack, in one hand a bundle, in the other a big stick.*

GRUSHA   (*Singing*)
           Four generals set off for Iran
           Four generals but not one man.
           The first did not strike a blow
           The second did not beat the foe
           For the third the weather was not right
           For the fourth the soldiers would not fight.
           Four generals went forth to attack
           Four generals turned back.

           Sosso Robakidse marched to Iran
           Sosso Robakidse was a man.
           He struck a sturdy blow
           He certainly beat the foe
           For him the weather was good enough
           For him the soldiers fought for love
           Sosso Robakidse marched to Iran
           Sosso Robakidse is our man.

           A peasant's cottage appears.

GRUSHA   (*to the child*) Noontime, eating time. Now we'll sit
           here quietly in the grass, while the good Grusha goes
           and buys a little jug of milk. (*She lays the child down
           and knocks at the cottage door. An old peasant
           opens it.*) Grandpa, could I have a little mug of milk?
           And perhaps a corn cake?

THE OLD MAN   Milk? We haven't any milk. The soldiers from the city
           took our goats. If you want milk, go to the soldiers.

GRUSHA   But Grandpa, you surely have a jug of milk for a child?

THE OLD MAN   And for a 'God Bless You', eh?

GRUSHA   Who said anything about a 'God Bless You'? (*She
           pulls out her purse.*) We're going to pay like princes.
           Head in the clouds, bottom in the water! (*The
           peasant goes off grumbling to fetch milk.*) And how
           much is this jug?

THE OLD MAN   Three piastres. Milk has gone up.

GRUSHA   Three piastres for that drop? (*Without a word* THE OLD
           MAN *slams the door in her face.*) Michael, did you
           hear that?

Three piastres! We can't afford that. (*She goes back, sits down again and gives the child her breast.*) Well, we must try again like this. Suck. Think of the three piastres. There's nothing there, but you think you're drinking, and that's something. (*Shaking her head, she realizes the child has stopped sucking. She gets up, walks back to the door, and knocks again.*) Open, Grandpa, we'll pay. (*Under her breath*) May God strike you! (*When* THE OLD MAN *appears again*) I thought it would be half a piastre. But the child must have something. What about one piastre?

THE OLD MAN Two.

GRUSHA Don't slam the door again. (*She rummages a long time in her purse.*) Here are two piastres. But this milk has got to last. We still have a long journey ahead of us. These are cut-throat prices. It's a sin.

THE OLD MAN If you want milk, kill the soldiers.

GRUSHA (*letting the child drink*) That's an expensive joke. Drink, Michael. This is half a week's pay. The people here think we've earned our money sitting on our bottom. Michael, Michael, I certainly took on a nice burden with you! (*Looking at the brocade coat in which the child is wrapped*) A brocade coat worth 1000 piastres, and not one piastre for milk. (*She glances round.*) Look! There's a carriage, with rich ladies. We ought to get on to that.

In front of a caravansary. GRUSHA *dressed in the brocade coat is seen approaching two elegant ladies. She holds the child in her arms.*

GRUSHA Oh, you ladies want to spend the night here too? It's awful how crowded it is everywhere! And not a carriage to be found! My coachman simply turned back. I've been walking half a mile on foot. Barefoot, too! My Persian shoes – you know those heels! But why doesn't someone come?

THE ELDER LADY That innkeeper certainly takes his time. The whole country has lost its manners since those goings-on started in the capital.

THE INNKEEPER *appears, a very dignified old man with a long beard, followed by his servant.*

THE INNKEEPER	Excuse an old man for keeping you waiting, ladies. My little grandchild was showing me a peach tree in blossom. There on the slope, beyond the cornfields. We're planting fruit trees there, a few cherries. Further west – (*pointing*) – the ground gets more stony. That's where the farmers graze their sheep. You ought to see the peach blossom, the pink is exquisite.
THE ELDER LADY	You live in a fertile region.
THE INNKEEPER	God has blessed it. How far on is the fruit-blossom further south, my ladies? I take it you come from the south?
THE YOUNGER LADY	I must admit I haven't been paying much attention to the landscape.
THE INNKEEPER	(*politely*) Of course, the dust. It is advisable to travel slowly on our high roads. Provided, of course, one isn't in too great a hurry.
THE ELDER LADY	Put your scarf round your throat, dearest. The evening breeze seems rather cool here.
THE INNKEEPER	It comes down from the Janga-Tau glaciers, my ladies.
GRUSHA	Yes, I'm afraid my son may catch cold.
THE ELDER LADY	A very spacious caravansary! Shall we go in?
THE INNKEEPER	Oh, the ladies want rooms? But the caravansary is full up, my ladies. And the servants have run off. I very much regret it, but I cannot accommodate another person, not even with references …
THE YOUNGER LADY	But we can't spend the night here on the road.
THE ELDER LADY	(*drily*) How much?
THE INNKEEPER	My ladies, you will understand that in these times, when so many fugitives, no doubt quite respectable people but not popular with the authorities, are looking for shelter, a house has to be particularly careful. Therefore …
THE ELDER LADY	My dear man, we aren't fugitives. We're simply moving to our summer residence in the mountains,

that's all. It would never occur to us to ask for
hospitality if – we needed it all that urgently.

THE INNKEEPER (*nodding his head in agreement*) Of course not.
I only doubt if the tiny room at my disposal
would suit the ladies. I have to charge 60
piastres per person. Are the ladies together?

GRUSHA In a way. I'm also in need of shelter.

THE YOUNGER 60 piastres! That's a cut-throat price.
LADY

THE INNKEEPER (*coldly*) My ladies, I have no desire to cut throats.
That's why ... (*He turns to go.*)

THE ELDER LADY Must we talk about throats? Let's go in. (*She enters,
followed by the servant.*)

THE YOUNGER (*desperate*) 180 piastres for one room! (*Glancing
LADY back at* GRUSHA) But with the child it's impossible!
What if it cries?

THE INNKEEPER The room costs 180, whether it's two persons or three.

THE YOUNGER (*changing her attitude to* GRUSHA) On the other hand, I
LADY couldn't bear to think of you on the road, my dear. Do come in.

*They enter the caravansary. From the rear on the
opposite side of the stage the servant appears with
some luggage. Behind him come* THE ELDER LADY, THE
YOUNGER LADY *and* GRUSHA *with the child.*

THE YOUNGER 180 piastres! I haven't been so upset since they
LADY brought dear Igor home.

THE ELDER LADY Must you talk about Igor?

THE YOUNGER Actually, we are four persons. The child is one too,
LADY isn't it? (*To* GRUSHA) Couldn't you pay half at least?

GRUSHA That's impossible. I had to leave in a hurry, you see.
And the Adjutant forgot to slip me enough money.

THE ELDER LADY Perhaps you haven't even got the 60?

GRUSHA That much I'll pay.

THE YOUNGER Where are the beds?
LADY

THE SERVANT There aren't any beds. Here are some sacks and
blankets. You'll have to arrange them yourselves. Be

glad you're not being put in a hole in the earth. Like lots of others. (*Exit.*)

THE YOUNGER LADY
Did you hear that? I'm going straight to the innkeeper. That man must be flogged.

THE ELDER LADY
Like your husband?

THE YOUNGER LADY
Don't be so cruel! (*She weeps.*)

THE ELDER LADY
How are we going to arrange something to sleep on?

GRUSHA
I'll see to that. (*She puts down the child.*) It's always easier when there are several hands. You still have the carriage. (*Sweeping the floor.*) I was taken completely by surprise. 'My dear Anastasia Katarinovska,' my husband was saying before luncheon, 'do go and lie down for a while. You know how easily you get migraine.' (*She spreads out sacks and makes beds. The ladies, watching her work, exchange glances.*) 'Georgi', said I to the Governor, 'I can't lie down when there are sixty for luncheon. And one can't trust the servants. And Michael Georgivich won't eat without me.' (*To Michael*) See, Michael? Everything'll be all right, what did I tell you! (*She suddenly realizes that the ladies are watching her strangely and whispering.*) Well, there we are! At least one doesn't have to lie on the bare floor. I've folded the blankets double.

THE ELDER LADY
(*imperiously*) You seem to be rather clever at making beds, my dear. Let's have a look at your hands!

GRUSHA
(*frightened*) What?

THE YOUNGER LADY
You're being asked to show your hands.

GRUSHA *shows the ladies her hands.*

THE YOUNGER LADY
(*triumphant*) Cracked! A servant!

THE ELDER LADY
(*goes to the door and shouts*) Service!

THE YOUNGER LADY
You're caught! You swindler! Just confess what mischief you're up to!

GRUSHA
(*confused*) I'm not up to any mischief. I just thought you might take us a little way in your carriage. Please, I ask you, don't make a noise, I'll go on my own.

THE YOUNGER LADY	(*while* THE ELDER LADY *continues shouting for service*) Yes, you'll go all right, but with the police. For the moment you'll stay. Don't you dare move, you!
GRUSHA	But I was ready to pay the 60 piastres. Here. (*She shows her purse.*) Look for yourself. I have them. Here are four tens, and here's a five – no, that's another ten, and ten, makes 60. All I want is to get the child on to the carriage. That's the truth.
THE YOUNGER LADY	Aha, so that's what you want. On to the carriage! Now it's come out.
GRUSHA	Madam, I confess, I am from humble family. Please don't call the police. The child is of noble birth, look at the linen. It's fleeing, like yourself.
THE YOUNGER LADY	Of noble birth! We know that one. The father's a prince, eh?
GRUSHA	(*to* THE ELDER LADY, *fiercely*) Stop shouting! Have you no heart at all?
THE YOUNGER LADY	(*to* THE ELDER LADY) Look out! She'll attack you! She's dangerous! Help! Murder!
THE SERVANT	(*entering*) What's going on here?
THE ELDER LADY	This person here had smuggled herself in by playing the lady. She's probably a thief.
THE YOUNGER LADY	And a dangerous one, too. She wanted to murder us. It's a case for the police. Oh God, I can feel my migraine coming on!
THE SERVANT	There aren't any police at the moment. (*To* GRUSHA) Pack up your things, sister, and make yourself scarce.
GRUSHA	(*angrily picking up the child*) You monsters! And they're already nailing your heads to the wall!
THE SERVANT	(*pushing her out*) Shut your trap. Or you'll have the Old Man here. And there's no trifling with him.
THE ELDER LADY	(*to* THE YOUNGER LADY) Just see if she hasn't stolen something already!
	While the ladies, right, look feverishly to see whether something has been stolen, THE SERVANT *and* GRUSHA *go out through the door, left.*

THE SERVANT   Look before you leap, I say. Another time have a good look at people before you get mixed up with them.

GRUSHA   I thought they'd be more likely to treat their own kind better.

THE SERVANT   Not them! Believe me, nothing's harder than aping a lazy useless person. Once they suspect you can wipe your own arse, or that your hands have ever touched a broom, the game's up. Just wait a minute. I'll get you a corn cake and a few apples.

GRUSHA   Better not. I must get out before the Old Man comes. And if I walk all night I'll be out of danger, I think. (*She walks away.*)

THE SERVANT   (*calling after her in a low voice*) At the next crossroads, turn right.

She disappears.

THE SINGER   As Grusha Vachnadze wandered northwards
She was followed by the Prince's Ironshirts.

THE MUSICIANS   How will the barefooted girl escape the Ironshirts
The bloodhounds, the trappers?
They are hunting even by night.
Pursuers don't get tired.
Butchers sleep little.

Two Ironshirts are trudging along the highway.

THE CORPORAL   Blockhead, you'll never amount to anything. Why? Because your heart's not in it. Your superior sees it in little things. Yesterday when I laid that fat woman, I admit you collared her husband as I commanded. And you did kick him in the stomach. But did you enjoy it like a good soldier? Or did you just do it from a sense of duty? I've kept my eyes on you, blockhead. You're like a hollow reed or a tinkling cymbal. You'll never get promoted. (*They walk awhile in silence.*) Don't you get the idea I don't notice how insubordinate you are in every way. I forbid you to limp! You do it simply because I sold the horses, and I

sold them because I'd never have got that price
again. I know you: you limp just to show me you
don't like marching. But that won't help you. It'll go
against you. Sing!

THE TWO
IRONSHIRTS

(*singing*)
O sadly one morning, one morning in May
I kissed my darling and rode far away.
Protect her, dear friends, until home from the wars
I come riding in triumph, alive on my horse.

THE CORPORAL   Louder!

THE TWO
IRONSHIRTS

When I lie in my grave and my sword turns to rust
My darling shall bring me a handful of dust.
For the feet that so gaily ran up to her door
And the arms that went round her shall please her
no more.

They begin to walk again in silence.

THE CORPORAL   A good soldier has his heart and soul in it. He lets
himself be hacked to pieces by his superiors and
even while dying he's aware of his Corporal nodding
approval. For him that's reward enough. That's all he
wants. But *you* won't get a nod. And you'll croak just
the same. Christ, how am I to lay my hands on the
Governor's bastard with an ass like you!

They trudge on.

THE SINGER   When Grusha Vachnadze came to the River Sirra
The flight grew too much for her, the helpless
child too heavy.

THE MUSICIANS   The rosy dawn in the cornfields
Is nothing but cold to the sleepless.
The gay clatter of the milk cans in the farmyard
Where the smoke rises is nothing but a threat to the
fugitives.
She who drags the child feels nothing but its
weight.

GRUSHA *stops in front of a farm.*

GRUSHA   Now you've wetted yourself again, and you know
              I've no nappies. Michael, we've got to part. This is far
              enough from the city. They won't want you so badly,
              little squit, that they'll follow you all this way. The
              woman looks kind, and just you smell the milk! So
              farewell, little Michael. I'll forget how you kicked me
              in the back all night to make me go faster. And you –
              you forget the meagre fare. It was meant well. I'd
              love to have kept you, because your nose is so small,
              but it can't be done. I'd have shown you your first
              rabbit and – how not to wet yourself, but I must turn
              back, because my sweetheart the soldier might soon
              return, and suppose he didn't find me? You can't ask
              that of me, Michael!

              A fat PEASANT WOMAN *carries a milk can to the door.*
              GRUSHA *waits until she has gone in, then gingerly*
              approaches the house. She tiptoes to the door and
              lays the child on the threshold. Then, hiding behind
              a tree, she waits until THE PEASANT WOMAN *opens the*
              door and sees the bundle.

THE PEASANT   Jesus Christ, what's this? Husband!
WOMAN

THE PEASANT   What's up? Let me have my soup.

THE PEASANT   (*to the child*) Where's your mother? Haven't you got
WOMAN   one? It's a boy. And the linen is fine, it's from a good
              family. And they just leave him on our doorstep. Oh,
              what times we live in!

THE PEASANT   If they think we're going to feed it, they're mistaken. You
              take it to the priest in the village. That's all we can do.

THE PEASANT   What will the priest do with it? It needs a mother.
WOMAN   There, it's waking up. Don't you think we could keep it?

THE PEASANT   (*shouting*) No!

THE PEASANT   I could lay it in the corner, next to the armchair. I only
WOMAN   need a crib for it. And I can take it into the fields with me.
              Look how it's smiling! Husband, we have a roof over our
              heads and we can do it. I won't hear another word.

              She carries the child into the house. THE PEASANT
              follows, protesting.

GRUSHA *steps out from behind the tree, laughs, and hurries away in the opposite direction.*

THE SINGER	Why so gay, you, making for home?
THE MUSICIANS	Because with a smile the child Has won new parents for himself, that's why I'm gay. Because I am rid of the loved one That's why I'm happy.
THE SINGER	And why are you sad?
THE MUSICIANS	I'm sad because I'm single and free Of the little burden in whom a heart was beating: Like one robbed, like one impoverished I'm going.

GRUSHA *walks for a short while, then meets the two Ironshirts, who hold her up at the point of a lance.*

THE CORPORAL Young lady, you're running into the Armed Forces. Where are you coming from? When are you coming? Are you entertaining illegal relations with the enemy? Where is he hiding? What sort of movements is he making in your rear? What about the hills? What about the valley? How are your stockings fastened?

GRUSHA *stands there frightened.*

GRUSHA They are strongly fastened; you'd better withdraw.

THE CORPORAL I always withdraw. In that respect I'm reliable. Why are you staring like that at the lance? In the field a soldier never loses control of his lance. That's an order. Learn it by heart, blockhead. Now then, young lady, where are you off to?

GRUSHA To my intended, one Simon Chachava, of the Palace Guard in Nukha. Wait till I write to him; he'll break your bones for you.

THE CORPORAL Simon Chachava? Indeed! I know him. He gave me the key so I could keep an eye on you once in a while. Blockhead, we're getting unpopular. We must make her realize we have honourable intentions. Young lady, my

apparent flippancy hides a serious nature. So I'll tell
you officially: I want a child from you.

GRUSHA *utters a little scream.*

Blockhead, she has understood. Ooh, isn't that a
sweet fright! 'But first I must take the bread out of
the oven, Officer! But first I must change my torn
chemise, Colonel!' But joking apart. Listen, young
lady, we are looking for a certain child in these parts.
Have you heard of a child from the city, of good
family, dressed in fine linen?

GRUSHA　　No. I've heard nothing.

THE SINGER　　Run, kind heart! The killers are coming!
Help the helpless child, helpless girl! And so she
runs.

*Suddenly, panic-stricken, she turns round and runs.
The Ironshirts glance at each other, then follow her,
cursing.*

THE MUSICIANS　　In the bloodiest times
There are still good people.

As GRUSHA *enters the cottage,* THE PEASANT WOMAN *is
bending over the child's crib.*

GRUSHA　　Hide it! Quick! The Ironshirts are coming! It was I
who laid it on your doorstep. But it isn't mine. It's of
a noble family.

THE PEASANT
WOMAN　　Who's coming? What sort of Ironshirts?

GRUSHA　　Don't ask questions. The Ironshirts who are looking
for it.

THE PEASANT
WOMAN　　They've no business in my house. But it seems I must
have a word with you.

GRUSHA　　Take off the fine linen. That will give us away.

THE PEASANT
WOMAN　　Oh, you and your linen! In this house I decide. And
don't you mess up my room. But why did you
abandon it? That's a sin.

GRUSHA　　(*looking out of the window*) There, they're coming
from behind the trees. I shouldn't have run away.
That gave them ideas. What on earth shall I do?

THE PEASANT WOMAN	(*looking out of the window and suddenly starting with fear*) Jesus and Mary! Ironshirts!
GRUSHA	They're after the child!
THE PEASANT WOMAN	But suppose they come in!
GRUSHA	You mustn't give it to them. Say it's yours.
THE PEASANT WOMAN	Yes.
GRUSHA	They'll run it through if you let them have it.
THE PEASANT WOMAN	But suppose they demand it? The money for the harvest is in the house.
GRUSHA	If you let them have it, they'll run it through, here in your room! You've got to say it's yours.
THE PEASANT WOMAN	Yes, but suppose they don't believe me?
GRUSHA	You must speak firmly.
THE PEASANT WOMAN	They'll burn the roof over our head.
GRUSHA	That's why you've got to say it's yours. His name's Michael. I shouldn't have told you that. THE PEASANT WOMAN *nods.* Don't nod your head like that. And don't tremble; they'll notice.
THE PEASANT WOMAN	Yes.
GRUSHA	Stop saying yes. I can't stand it any longer. (*She shakes her.*) Haven't *you* got a child?
THE PEASANT WOMAN	(*muttering*) In the war.
GRUSHA	Then perhaps he's an Ironshirt, too, by now? And what if he ran children through? You'd give him a fine piece of your mind! 'Stop waving that lance in my room! Is that what I've reared you for? Go and wash your neck before you speak to your mother.'
THE PEASANT WOMAN	That's true, I wouldn't let him behave like that.
GRUSHA	Promise me you'll say it's yours.
THE PEASANT WOMAN	Yes
GRUSHA	There! They're coming!

There is a knocking at the door. The women don't answer. Enter the Ironshirts. THE PEASANT WOMAN *bows deeply.*

THE CORPORAL	Well, there she is. What did I tell you? My nose. I smelled her. Young lady, I have a question to ask you: Why did you run away? What did you think I would do to you? I'll bet it was something lewd. Confess!
GRUSHA	(*while* THE PEASANT WOMAN *continues to bow*) I'd left the milk on the stove. Then I suddenly remembered it.
THE CORPORAL	I thought it was because you imagined I'd looked at you in a lewd way – as if I were thinking there could be something between us. A lustful glance, know what I mean?
GRUSHA	I didn't see that.
THE CORPORAL	But it could have been, eh? You must admit that. After all, I could be a swine. I'm quite frank with you: I could think of all sorts of things if we were alone. (*To* THE PEASANT WOMAN) Haven't you got something to do in the yard? The chickens to feed?
THE PEASANT WOMAN	(*falling suddenly to her knees*) Soldier, I didn't know anything about it. Please don't set my house on fire.
THE CORPORAL	What are you talking about?
THE PEASANT WOMAN	I have nothing to do with it. She left it on the doorstep, I swear.
THE CORPORAL	(*suddenly sees the child and whistles*) Ah, there's a little one in the crib! Blockhead, I smell a thousand piastres. Take the old girl out and hold on to her. It looks as though I'll have to do some cross-examining.
	THE PEASANT WOMAN *lets herself be led by the soldier, without a word.*
	Well, there's the child I wanted to have from you. (*He walks towards the crib.*)
GRUSHA	Officer, it's mine. It's not the one you're after.
THE CORPORAL	I'll just have a look at it. (*He bends over the crib.* GRUSHA *looks round in despair.*)
GRUSHA	It's mine! It's mine!
THE CORPORAL	Nice linen!
	GRUSHA *jumps at him to pull him away. He throws her off and again bends over the crib.* *Looking round in despair, she suddenly*

sees a big log of wood, seizes it in panic, and hits
THE CORPORAL *over the head from behind. She quickly*
picks up the child and dashes off.

THE SINGER

After her escape from the Ironshirts
After twenty-two days of wandering
At the foot of the Janga-Tau glacier
From this moment Grusha Vachnadze decided to
be the child's mother.

THE MUSICIANS

The helpless girl
Became the mother of the helpless child.

GRUSHA *squats over a half-frozen stream to ladle*
some water in her hand for the child.

GRUSHA

Nobody wants to take you
So I shall have to take you
There is no one else but me, my dear
On this black day in a meagre year
Who will not forsake you.

Since I've carried you too long
And with sore feet
Since the milk was too dear
I grew fond of you.
(I wouldn't be without you any more.)

I'll throw your fine little shirt away
And wrap you in rags
I'll wash you and christen you
With glacier water.
(You'll have to bear it.)

She has taken off the child's fine linen and wrapped
it in a rag.

THE SINGER

When Grusha Vachnadze, pursued by the
Ironshirts
Came to the narrow footbridge of the Eastern slope
She sang the song of the rotten bridge
And risked two lives.

A wind has risen. The bridge on the glacier is visible in the semi-darkness. One rope is broken, and half the bridge is hanging down the precipice. Merchants, two men and a woman, stand undecided before the bridge as GRUSHA *and the child arrive. One man is trying to retrieve a hanging rope with a stick.*

THE FIRST MAN   Take your time, young woman. You won't get over that pass anyway.

GRUSHA   But I simply have to get my child over to the east side. To my brother.

THE MERCHANT WOMAN   Have to? What d'you mean by have to? I have to get there, too – because I have to buy two carpets in Atum – carpets a woman had to sell because her husband had to die. But can I do what I have to; can she? Andrei has been fishing for two hours for that rope. And I ask you, how are we to fasten it, even if he gets it?

THE FIRST MAN   (*listening*) Shush, I think I hear something.

GRUSHA   The bridge is not quite rotten. I think I'll try and cross it.

THE MERCHANT WOMAN   I wouldn't try that even if the devil himself were after me. It's suicide.

THE FIRST MAN   (*shouting*) Hi!

GRUSHA   Don't shout! (*To* THE MERCHANT WOMAN.) Tell him not to shout.

THE FIRST MAN   But someone down there's calling. Perhaps they've lost their way.

THE MERCHANT WOMAN   And why shouldn't he shout? Is there something wrong with you? Are they after you?

GRUSHA   Well, I'll have to tell you. Ironshirts are after me. I knocked one down.

THE SECOND MAN   Hide our merchandise!

The woman hides a sack behind a rock.

THE FIRST MAN   Why didn't you tell us that at once? (*To the other*) If they catch her they'll make mincemeat out of her!

GRUSHA   Get out of my way. I've got to cross that bridge.

THE SECOND MAN   You can't. There's a precipice of two thousand feet.

THE FIRST MAN   Even if we could get the rope it wouldn't make sense. We could hold it with our hands, but then the Ironshirts could get across in the same way.

GRUSHA   Out of my way.

Shouts from a distance: 'Let's get up there!'

THE MERCHANT WOMAN   They're getting near. But you can't take the child across that bridge. It's sure to break. Just look down!

GRUSHA *looks down the precipice. The Ironshirts are heard shouting below.*

THE SECOND MAN   Two thousand feet!

GRUSHA   But those men are worse.

THE FIRST MAN   Anyway you can't do it with the child. Risk your own life if they are after you, but not the child's.

THE SECOND MAN   She's even heavier with the child.

THE MERCHANT WOMAN   Perhaps she's really got to go. Give it to me. I'll hide it and you cross the bridge alone.

GRUSHA   I won't. We belong together. (*To the child*) Live together, die together. (*She sings*)

> If the gulf is deep
> And the rotten bridge sways
> It is not for us, son
> To choose our ways.
>
> The way that I know
> Is the one for your feet
> The bread that I find
> Is all you will eat.
>
> Of every four morsels
> You shall have three.
> I would that I knew
> How big they will be!
> I'll try it.

THE MERCHANT WOMAN   That's tempting God.

Shouts from beneath.

GRUSHA   I beg you, throw that stick away, or they'll get the rope and follow me.

She starts off on to the swinging bridge. THE MERCHANT WOMAN *screams when the bridge looks like breaking. But* GRUSHA *walks on and reaches the far side.*

THE FIRST MAN   She's done it!

THE MERCHANT WOMAN   (*who has fallen on her knees and begun to pray, angrily*) But I still think it was a sin.

The Ironshirts appear, the Corporal's head bandaged.

THE CORPORAL   Have you seen a woman with a child?

THE FIRST MAN   (*while the second throws away his stick*) Yes, there she is! But the bridge won't carry you!

THE CORPORAL   Blockhead, you'll suffer for this!

GRUSHA, *from the far bank, laughs and shows the child to the Ironshirts. She walks on. The bridge is left behind. Wind.*

GRUSHA   (*to the child*) You mustn't mind the wind. It's only a poor wretch, too. It has to push the clouds, and it feels the cold more than any of us. (*Snow starts falling.*) And the snow isn't the worst, Michael. It covers the little fir trees, so that they won't die in winter. And now I'll sing you a little song. Listen! (*She sings*)

> Your father's a thief
> Your mother's a whore:
> All the nice people
> Will love you therefore.
>
> The son of the tiger
> Brings the foals their feed
> The snake-child milk
> To mothers in need.

4

In the Northern Mountains

THE SINGER	Seven days the sister wandered
	Across the glacier, down the hills she wandered.
	'When I enter my brother's house', she thought to herself
	'He will rise and embrace me'.
	'Is that you, sister?' he will say
	'I have been expecting you for so long. This here is my dear wife.
	And this is my farm, come to me by marriage.
	With eleven horses and thirty-one cows. Sit down.
	Sit down with your child at our table and eat.'
	The brother's house was in a lovely valley.
	When the sister came to the brother she was ill from her wanderings.
	The brother rose from the table.

A fat peasant couple who have just sat down to a meal. LAVRENTI VACHNADZE *already has a napkin round his neck, as* GRUSHA, *pale and supported by a* STABLEMAN, *enters with the child.*

LAVRENTI	Where do you come from, Grusha?
GRUSHA	(*feebly*) I've walked across the Janga-Tau Pass, Lavrenti.
STABLEMAN	I found her in front of the hay barn. She has a child with her.
THE SISTER-IN-LAW	Go and groom the roan. (*Exit* STABLEMAN.)
LAVRENTI	This is my wife, Aniko.
THE SISTER-IN-LAW	We thought you were in service in Nukha.
GRUSHA	(*barely able to stand*) Yes, I was there.
THE SISTER-IN-LAW	Wasn't it a good job? We were told it was a good one.
GRUSHA	The Governor has been killed.

LAVRENTI	Yes, we heard there were riots. Your aunt told us about it. Remember, Aniko?
THE SISTER-IN-LAW	Here, with us, it's quiet. City people always need some kind of excitement. (*She walks towards the door and shouts.*) Sosso, Sosso, take the flat cake out of the oven, d'you hear? Where are you? (*Exit, shouting.*)
LAVRENTI	(*quietly, quickly*) Has it got a father? (*As she shakes her head*) I thought so. We must think up something. She's very pious.
THE SISTER-IN-LAW	(*returning*) These servants! (*To* GRUSHA)You have a child?
GRUSHA	It's mine. (*She collapses.* LAVRENTI *helps her up.*)
THE SISTER-IN-LAW	Mary and Joseph, she's ill – what are we to do?

LAVRENTI *tries to lead* GRUSHA *to the bench by the store.* ANIKO *waves her away in horror and points to the sack by the wall.*

LAVRENTI	(*escorting her to the wall*) Sit down, sit down. I think it's just weakness.
THE SISTER-IN-LAW	As long as it's not scarlet fever.
LAVRENTI	Then she'd have spots. I'm sure it's only weakness. Don't worry, Aniko. (*To* GRUSHA) Do you feel better sitting?
THE SISTER-IN-LAW	Is the child hers?
GRUSHA	It's mine.
LAVRENTI	She's on her way to her husband.
THE SISTER-IN-LAW	Really? Your meat's getting cold. (LAVRENTI *sits down and begins to eat.*) Cold food's not good for you. At least the fat parts mustn't get cold; you know your stomach's your weak spot. (*To* GRUSHA) If your husband's not in town, where is he then?
LAVRENTI	She got married on the other side of the mountain, she says.
THE SISTER-IN-LAW	Oh, on the other side. (*She also sits down to eat.*)
GRUSHA	I think I'll have to lie down somewhere, Lavrenti.
THE SISTER-IN-LAW	(*goes on questioning her*) If it's consumption we'll all get it. Has your husband a farm?

GRUSHA	He's a soldier.
LAVRENTI	But he's coming into a farm – a small farm from his father.
THE SISTER-IN-LAW	Isn't he in the war? Why not?
GRUSHA	(*wearily*) Yes, he's in the war.
THE SISTER-IN-LAW	Then why d'you want to go to the farm?
LAVRENTI	When he comes back from the war, he'll come to his farm.
THE SISTER-IN-LAW	But you're going there now?
LAVRENTI	Yes, to wait for him.
THE SISTER-IN-LAW	(*shrilly*) Sosso, the cake!
GRUSHA	(*murmurs in fever*) A farm – a soldier – waiting – sit down – eat.
THE SISTER-IN-LAW	That's scarlet fever.
GRUSHA	(*starting up*) Yes, he has a farm!
LAVRENTI	I think it must be weakness, Aniko. Wouldn't you like to go and look after the cake yourself, my dear?
THE SISTER-IN-LAW	But when will he come back if the war, as they say, has broken out again? (*Waddling away, shouting*) Sosso! Where are you? Sosso!
LAVRENTI	(*getting up quickly and going to* GRUSHA) You'll get a bed in a moment. She has a good heart. But only after supper.
GRUSHA	(*holding out the child to him*) Take it. (*He takes it, looking anxiously round.*)
LAVRENTI	But you can't stay here long. You must realize she's very pious.

GRUSHA *collapses.* LAVRENTI *takes hold of her.*

THE SINGER	The sister was too ill.
	The cowardly brother had to give her shelter.
	The autumn passed, the winter came.
	The winter was long
	The winter was short.
	The people mustn't know.
	The rats mustn't bite
	The spring mustn't come.

GRUSHA *sits bent at the weaving loom in the scullery.*
She and the child, who squats on the floor, are
wrapped in blankets.

GRUSHA   (*sings while weaving*)

> Then the lover started to leave
> Then his girl ran pleading after him
> Pleading and crying, crying and pleading:
> Dearest mine, dearest mine
> As you now go into battle
> As you now have to fight the enemy
> Don't throw yourself into the front line
> And don't push with the rear line.
> In front is red fire
> In the rear is red smoke.
> Stay wisely in between
> Keep near the standard bearer.
> The first ones always die
> The last ones are also hit
> Those in the centre come home.

Michael, we must be clever. If we make ourselves
really small, like cockroaches, our sister-in-law will
forget we're in the house. Then we can stay here till
the snow melts. And don't cry because of the cold.
Being poor and cold as well puts people off.

Enter LAVRENTI. *He sits down beside* GRUSHA.

LAVRENTI   Why are you two sitting there muffled up like
coachmen? Perhaps it's too cold in the room?

GRUSHA   (*hastily removing her shawl*) It's not too cold, Lavrenti.

LAVRENTI   If it's too cold, you oughtn't sit here with the child.
Aniko would blame herself. (*Pause.*) I hope the
priest didn't question you about the child.

GRUSHA   He did, but I didn't tell him anything.

LAVRENTI   That's good. I wanted to talk to you about Aniko. She has
a good heart – but she's very, very sensitive. People only
have to mention our farm and she's worried. She takes
everything to heart, you know. Our milkmaid once went
to church with a hole in her stocking. Ever since then my

dear Aniko has always worn two pairs of stockings to church. It's hard to believe, but it's the old family in her. (*He listens.*) Are you sure there are no rats here? If so, you couldn't stay here. (*Sounds of drops from the roof.*) What's that dripping?

GRUSHA   Must be a barrel leaking.

LAVRENTI   Yes, it must be a barrel. Now you've already been here six months, haven't you? Was I talking about Aniko? Of course I didn't mention the Ironshirt. She has a weak heart. That's why she doesn't know you can't look for work. And that's why she made those remarks yesterday. (*They listen again to the melting snow.*) Can you believe it? She's worrying about your soldier. 'Suppose he comes back and doesn't find her!' she says, and lies awake. 'He can't come before the spring,' I tell her. The dear woman! (*The drops begin to fall faster.*) When d'you think he'll come? What's your idea? (GRUSHA *is silent.*) Not before the spring. That's what you think, too? (GRUSHA *is silent.*) I see you no longer believe he'll come back. (GRUSHA *does not answer.*) But when spring comes and the snow is melting on the passes you must leave here. Because then they can come and look for you. People are already talking about a child with an unmarried mother.

The beat of the falling drops has grown faster and steadier. Grusha, the snow is melting on the roof and spring is here.

GRUSHA   Yes.

LAVRENTI   (*eagerly*) Let me tell you what we'll do. You need a place to go to. And because of the child – (*he sighs*) – you must have a husband, to stop people talking. I've made cautious inquiries about how we can get a husband for you, Grusha, and I've found one. I talked to a woman who has a son, just over the mountain, a little farm. She's willing.

GRUSHA   But I can't marry another man! I must wait for Simon Chachava.

LAVRENTI   Of course. That's all been considered. You don't need a man in bed, but a man on paper. And that's the very

man I've found. The son of the woman I spoke to is
dying. Isn't that wonderful? He's just at his last gasp.
And everything's as we have said. A man just over the
mountain! And when you reached him he died, and
so you're a widow. What do you say?

GRUSHA   I could do with a stamped up document for Michael.

LAVRENTI   A stamp makes all the difference. Without a stamp
even the Shah of Persia couldn't prove he is the Shah.
And you'll have a roof over your head.

GRUSHA   How much does she want for it?

LAVRENTI   400 piastres.

GRUSHA   Where will you find the money?

LAVRENTI   (*guiltily*) Aniko's milk money.

GRUSHA   No-one will know us over there. I'll do it.

LAVRENTI   (*gets up*) I'll tell the woman at once. (*Exit quickly.*)

GRUSHA   Michael, you cause a lot of trouble. I came by you as
the pear tree comes by the sparrows. And because a
Christian bends down and picks up a crust of bread
so it won't go to waste. Michael, I ought to have
walked away quickly on that Easter Sunday in Nukha.
Now I'm the fool.

THE SINGER   The bridegroom was lying on his deathbed, when
the bride arrived.
The bridegroom's mother was waiting at the door,
biding them hurry.
The bride brought along a child, the witness hid it
during the wedding.

*A space divided by a partition. On one side a bed.
Under the mosquito-net lies a very sick man. On the
other side the* MOTHER-IN-LAW *rushes in pulling* GRUSHA
after her. They are followed by LAVRENTI *and the child.*

THE MOTHER-IN-
LAW   Quick! Quick! Or he'll die on us before the wedding.
(*To* LAVRENTI) But I was never told she already had a
child.

LAVRENTI   What's it matter? (*Pointing towards the dying man*)
It's all the same to him in his condition.

THE MOTHER-IN-LAW	Him? But I won't survive the shame. We're honest people. (*She begins to weep.*) My Yussup doesn't have to marry someone who already has a child.
LAVRENTI	All right, I'll add another 200 piastres. You have it in writing that the farm will go to you; but she has the right to live here for two years.
THE MOTHER-IN-LAW	(*drying her tears*) It will hardly cover the funeral expenses. I hope she will really lend me a hand with the work. And now what's happened to the monk? He must have slipped out by the kitchen window. When they get wind in the village that Yussup's end is near, they'll all be round our necks. Oh dear! I'll go and get the monk. But he mustn't see the child.
LAVRENTI	I'll take care he doesn't see it. But why a monk? Why not a priest?
THE MOTHER-IN-LAW	Oh, he's just as good. I made one mistake. I paid him half his fee in advance. Now he'll have gone to the tavern. I hope … (*She runs off.*)
LAVRENTI	She saved on the priest, the wretch! She's hired a cheap monk.
GRUSHA	Send Simon Chachava to me if he turns up.
LAVRENTI	Yes. (*Glancing at the sick man*) Won't you have a look at him?

GRUSHA, *taking Michael to her, shakes her head.*

He's not moving an eyelid. I hope we aren't too late.

They listen. On the opposite side enter neighbours, who look round and take up positions against the walls. They start muttering prayers. Enter THE MOTHER-IN-LAW *with* THE MONK.

THE MOTHER-IN-LAW	(*surprised and angry, to* THE MONK) Now we're for it! (*She bows to the guests.*) I must ask you to wait a few moments. My son's bride has just arrived from town and we've got to have an emergency wedding. (*She goes with* THE MONK *into the bedchamber.* I knew you'd spread it about. (*To* GRUSHA) The wedding can start at once. Here's the licence. I and the bride's brother – (LAVRENTI *tries to hide in the background, after having quickly taken Michael away from* GRUSHA.)

(THE MOTHER-IN-LAW *beckons him away from the child*)
– the bride's brother and I are the witnesses.

GRUSHA *has bowed to* THE MONK. *They approach the bed:*
THE MOTHER-IN-LAW *lifts the mosquito-net:* THE MONK *begins babbling the marriage service in Latin. Meanwhile* THE MOTHER-IN-LAW *beckons to* LAVRENTI *to get rid of the child, but* LAVRENTI, *fearing that the child will cry, draws its attention to the ceremony.* GRUSHA *glances once at the child, and* LAVRENTI *makes the child wave to her.*

THE MONK	Are you prepared to be a faithful, obedient and good wife to this man? And to cleave to him until death you do part?
GRUSHA	(*looking at the child*) Yes.
THE MONK	(*to the dying man*) And are you prepared to be a good and loving husband to your wife until death you do part?

As the dying man does not answer, THE MONK *repeats the question, then looks round.*

THE MOTHER-IN-LAW	Of course he is! Didn't you hear him say yes?
THE MONK	All right. We declare this marriage contracted. Now what about Extreme Unction?
THE MOTHER-IN-LAW	Nothing doing! The wedding was quite expensive enough. I must now take care of the mourners. (*To* LAVRENTI) Did we say 700?
LAVRENTI	600. (*He pays.*) Now I don't want to sit and get acquainted with the guests. So farewell, Grusha. And if my widowed sister comes to visit me one day, she'll get a 'welcome' from my wife. Or I'll get disagreeable.

He leaves. The mourners glance after him without interest.

THE MONK	And may one ask whose this child is?
THE MOTHER-IN-LAW	Is there a child? I don't see any child. And you don't see one either – understand? Or else I've seen all kinds of things happening behind the tavern! Come along now.

They move back to the room. After GRUSHA *has put down the child and told it to be quiet, she is introduced to the neighbours.*

This is my daughter-in-law. She arrived just in time to find dear Yussup still alive.

ONE OF THE WOMEN	He's been ill now a whole year, hasn't he? When my Vassili was called up he was there to say goodbye.
ANOTHER WOMAN	Such things are terrible for a farm. With the corn ripe on the stalk and the farmer in bed! It will be a blessing for him if he doesn't suffer much longer, I say.
FIRST WOMAN	(*confidentially*) At first we thought he took to his bed because of military service, you know. And now his end is coming.
THE MOTHER-IN-LAW	Please sit down and have some cakes.

She beckons to GRUSHA *and both women go into the bedroom, where they pick up trays of cakes from the floor. The guests, among them* THE MONK, *sit on the floor and begin conversing in subdued voices.*

A VERY OLD PEASANT	(*to whom* THE MONK *has slipped the bottle he has taken from his cassock*) There's a little one, you say! How can Yussup have managed that?
THIRD WOMAN	Anyway, she was lucky to have brought it off in time, with him so sick.
THE MOTHER-IN-LAW	They are gossiping already. And stuffing themselves with the funeral cakes at the same time. And if he doesn't die today, I'll have to bake fresh ones tomorrow.
GRUSHA	I'll bake them.
THE MOTHER-IN-LAW	When some riders passed by last night, and I went out to see who they were, he was lying there like a corpse! That's why I sent for you. It can't take much longer. (*She listens.*)
THE MONK	Dear wedding guests and mourners! We stand deeply moved in front of a bed of death and marriage, because the bride gets into bed and the groom into the grave. The groom is already washed and the bride is already hot. For in the marriage-bed lies the last Will, and that makes people randy. Oh, my children, how varied is the fate of man! The one dies to get a roof over his head, and the other marries so that flesh may be turned to dust, from which it was made. Amen.
THE MOTHER-IN-LAW	(*who had listened*) He's got his own

back. I shouldn't have hired such a cheap one. That's what you'd expect. An expensive one knows how to behave. In Sura there's one who is even in the odour of sanctity; but of course he charges a fortune. A fifty-piastre priest like this one here has no dignity. And as for piety, he has precisely fifty piastres' worth, and no more. And when I fetched him from the tavern he was just finishing a speech and shouting: 'The war is over, beware of the peace!' We must go in.

GRUSHA   (*giving Michael a cake*) Eat this cake and be a good boy, Michael. We are respectable now.

The two women carry the trays of cakes to the guests. The dying man is sitting up in bed: he puts his head out from under the mosquito-net and watches the two women. Then he sinks back again. THE MONK *takes two bottles from his cassock and offers them to the peasant behind him. Enter three musicians, to whom* THE MONK *waves with a grin.*

THE MOTHER-IN-LAW   (*to the musicians*) What have you got your instruments for?

A MUSICIAN   Brother Anastasius here – (*pointing at* THE MONK) – told us there was a wedding going on.

THE MOTHER-IN-LAW   What! You brought them? Three more on my neck! Don't you know there's a dying man next door?

THE MONK   That's a tempting task for an artist. They could play a hushed Wedding March or a gay Funeral Dance.

THE MOTHER-IN-LAW   Well, you might as well play. I can't stop you eating, in any case.

The musicians play a musical medley. The women offer cakes.

THE MONK   The trumpet sounds like a whining baby. And you, little drum, what gossip are you spreading abroad?

A PEASANT   (*beside* THE MONK) What about the bride shaking a leg?

THE MONK   Shake the legs or rattle the bones?

THE PEASANT   (*beside* THE MONK, *singing*)

    When pretty Miss Plushbottom wed
    A rich man with no teeth in his head

They enquired, 'Is it fun?'
She replied, 'No, it's none.
Still, there're candles and soon he'll be dead.'

THE MOTHER-IN-LAW *throws the drunken man out. The music stops.* THE GUESTS *are embarrassed. Pause.*

THE GUESTS   (*loudly*) Have you heard the latest? The Grand Duke's back! – But the Princes are against him. – Oh, the Shah of Persia, they say, has lent him a great army, to restore order in Grusinia. – How is this possible? After all, the Shah of Persia is against the Grand Duke! – But against disorder, too. – In any case, the war's over. Our soldiers are already coming back.

GRUSHA *drops the tray of cakes.*

AN OLD WOMAN   (*to* GRUSHA) Are you feeling ill? That's just excitement about dear Yussup. Sit down and rest awhile, my dear.

GRUSHA *stands, swaying.*

THE GUESTS   Now everything will be as it was. Only the taxes will go up because we'll have to pay for the war.

GRUSHA   (*weakly*) Did someone say the soldiers are back?

A MAN   I did.

GRUSHA   That can't be true.

THE MAN   (*to a woman*) Show her the shawl. We bought it from a soldier. It's from Persia.

GRUSHA   (*looking at the shawl*) They are here.

A long pause. GRUSHA *kneels as if to pick up the cakes. As she does so she takes the silver cross and chain out of her blouse, kisses it, and starts praying.*

THE MOTHER-IN-LAW   (*while the guests silently watch* GRUSHA) What's the matter with you? Won't you look after our guests? What's all this nonsense from the city got to do with us?

THE GUESTS   (*resuming their conversation while* GRUSHA *remains with her forehead bent to the ground*) Persian saddles can be bought from soldiers, but some exchange them for crutches. – Only one side's bigwigs can win, but the soldiers on both sides are the losers. – At least the war's over now.

It's something that they can't call you up any more. –
(*The dying man sits bolt upright in bed. He listens.*)
What we need most are two weeks of good weather.
– There's hardly a pear on our trees this year.

THE MOTHER-IN-LAW (*offering the cakes*) Have some more cake. And
enjoy it. There's more to come.

*THE MOTHER-IN-LAW goes to the bedroom with empty
trays. Unaware of the dying man, she bends down
to pick up some more cakes, when he begins to talk
in a hoarse voice.*

YUSSUP How many more cakes are you going to stuff down
their throats? D'you think I can shit money? (THE
MOTHER-IN-LAW *starts, and stares at him aghast, while
he puts his head out from behind the mosquito-net.*)
Did they say the war was over?

FIRST WOMAN (*talking kindly to* GRUSHA *in the next room*) Has the
young woman someone in the war?

THE MAN That's good news that they're on their way home, eh?

YUSSUP Don't stare so! Where's the wife you've foisted on me?

*Receiving no answer, he climbs out of bed and in
his nightshirt staggers past his mother into the
other room. Trembling, she follows him with the
cake tray.*

THE GUESTS (*seeing him and shrieking*) Jesus, Mary and Joseph! Yussup!

*Everyone leaps up in alarm. The women rush to the
door.* GRUSHA, *still on her knees, turns round and
stares at the man.*

YUSSUP The funeral supper! That's what you'd like! Get out
before I kick you out!

THE GUESTS *stampede from the house.*

YUSSUP (*grumpily to* GRUSHA) That puts a spoke in your wheel, eh?

*Receiving no answer, he turns round and takes a
cake from the tray which his mother holds.*

THE SINGER Oh, confusion! The wife discovers that she has a
husband!
By day there's the child, by night there's the man.

The lover is on his way day and night.
The married couple are looking at each other. The
chamber is narrow.

YUSSUP *sits naked in a high wooden bathtub. His*
mother pours water from a jug. Next door in the
bedroom GRUSHA *squats with Michael, who is*
playing at mending a straw mat.

YUSSUP That's her business, not yours. Where's she hiding now?

THE MOTHER-IN-LAW (*calling*) Grusha! The peasant wants you!

GRUSHA (*to Michael*) There are still two holes to mend.

YUSSUP (*as* GRUSHA *enters*) Scrub my back!

GRUSHA Can't the peasant do that himself?

YUSSUP 'Can't the peasant do that himself?' Get the brush! To
hell with you! Are you the wife or are you a stranger?
(*To* THE MOTHER-IN-LAW) Too cold!

THE MOTHER-IN-LAW I'll run and get some more hot water.

GRUSHA Let me do it.

YUSSUP You stay here. (THE MOTHER-IN-LAW *goes out.*) Rub
harder. And don't make such a fuss. You've seen a
naked man before. That child of yours can't have
come out of thin air.

GRUSHA The child was not conceived in joy, if that's what the
peasant means.

YUSSUP (*turning and grinning*) A likely story! (GRUSHA *stops*
scrubbing him and starts back. Enter THE
MOTHER-IN-LAW.) This is a nice thing you've saddled me
with here! A cold-fish for a wife!

THE MOTHER-IN-LAW She isn't willing.

YUSSUP Pour – but go easy! Ow! Go easy, I said. (*To* GRUSHA.)
I'd be surprised if you hadn't been up to something in
the city. What else would you be here for? But I won't
say anything about that. I also haven't said anything
about the bastard you brought into my house. But my
patience with you is coming to an end. It's against
nature. (*To* THE MOTHER-IN-LAW) More! (*To* GRUSHA) And
even if your soldier does return, you're married.

GRUSHA   Yes.

YUSSUP   But your soldier won't return now. Don't you believe it.

GRUSHA   No.

YUSSUP   You're cheating me. You're my wife and you're not
my wife. Where you lie, nothing lies. And yet no
other woman can lie there. When I go to work in the
mornings I'm dead tired. When I lie down at night
I'm awake as the devil. God has made you a woman,
and what d'you do about it? My fields don't bring me
in enough to buy myself a woman in town. Besides,
it's a long way. Woman hoes the fields and parts her
legs. That's what our almanac says. D'you hear?

GRUSHA   Yes. (*Quietly*) I don't like cheating you out of it.

YUSSUP   She doesn't like! Pour some more water. (THE
MOTHER-IN-LAW *pours*.) Ow!

THE SINGER   As she sat by the stream to wash the linen
She saw his image in the water, and his face grew
dimmer
As the months passed by.
As she raised herself to wring the linen
She heard his voice from the murmuring maple,
and his voice grew fainter
As the months passed by.
Excuses and sighs grew more numerous, tears and
sweat flowed faster
As the months passed by, as the child grew up.

GRUSHA *sits by a stream dipping linen into the water.
Some distance away a few children are standing.*
GRUSHA *is talking to Michael.*

GRUSHA   You can play with them, Michael. But don't let them
order you about because you're the smallest.

MICHAEL *nods and joins the children. They start playing.*

THE TALLEST BOY   Today we're going to play Heads-off. (*To a fat boy*)
You're the Prince and you must laugh. (*To* MICHAEL)
You're the Governor. (*To a girl*) You're
the Governor's wife and you cry when
his head's chopped off. And I do the

chopping. (*He shows his wooden sword.*) With this. First, the Governor's led into the courtyard. The Prince walks ahead. The Governor's wife comes last.

They form a procession. THE FAT BOY *goes ahead, and laughs. Then comes* MICHAEL, *and* THE TALLEST BOY, *and then* THE GIRL, *who weeps.*

MICHAEL	(*standing still*) Me too chop head off!
THE TALLEST BOY	That's my job. You're the smallest. The Governor's part is the easiest. All you do is kneel down and have your head chopped off. That's simple.
MICHAEL	Me too have sword.
THE TALLEST BOY	That's mine. (*He gives him a kick.*)
THE GIRL	(*shouting to* GRUSHA) He doesn't want to do what he's told.
GRUSHA	(*laughing*) Even ducklings take to water, they say.
THE TALLEST BOY	You can play the Prince if you know how to laugh. MICHAEL *shakes his head.*
THE FAT BOY	I'm the best laugher. Let him chop off the head just once. Then you do it, then me.

Reluctantly THE TALLEST BOY *hands* MICHAEL *the wooden sword and kneels.* THE FAT BOY *sits down, smacks his thigh and laughs with all his might.* THE GIRL *weeps loudly.* MICHAEL *swings the big sword and chops off the head. In doing so he topples over.*

THE TALLEST BOY	Hi, I'll show you how to do it properly.

MICHAEL *runs away, and the children run after him.* GRUSHA *laughs, following them with her eyes. On turning round, she sees* SIMON CHACHAVA *standing on the opposite bank. He wears a shabby uniform.*

GRUSHA	Simon!
SIMON	Is that Grusha Vachnadze?
GRUSHA	Simon!
SIMON	(*politely*) A good morning, and good health to the young lady.
GRUSHA	(*gets up gaily and bows deeply*) A good morning to the soldier. And thank God he has returned in good health.
SIMON	They found better fish than me, so they didn't eat me, said the haddock.

GRUSHA   Courage, said the kitchen boy. Luck, said the hero.

SIMON   And how are things here? Was the winter bearable? Did the neighbour behave?

GRUSHA   The winter was a little rough, the neighbour as usual, Simon.

SIMON   May one ask if a certain person is still in the habit of putting her leg in the water when washing her linen?

GRUSHA   The answer is no. Because of the eyes in the bushes.

SIMON   The young lady is talking about soldiers. Here stands a paymaster.

GRUSHA   Is that worth twenty piastres?

SIMON   And board.

GRUSHA   (*with tears in her eyes*) Behind the barracks under the date trees.

SIMON   Just there. I see someone has kept her eyes open.

GRUSHA   Someone has.

SIMON   And has not forgotten. (GRUSHA *shakes her head.*) And so the door is still on its hinges, as they say. (GRUSHA *looks at him in silence and shakes her head again.*) What's that mean? Is something wrong?

GRUSHA   Simon Chachava, I can never go back to Nukha. Something has happened.

SIMON   What has happened?

GRUSHA   It so happened that I knocked down an Ironshirt.

SIMON   Grusha Vachnadze will have had her reasons for that.

GRUSHA   Simon Chachava, my name is also no longer what it was.

SIMON   (*after a pause*) I don't understand that.

GRUSHA   When do women change their names, Simon? Let me explain it to you: Nothing stands between us. Everything between us has remained as it was. You've got to believe that.

SIMON   How can nothing stand between us and things be changed?

GRUSHA   How can I explain it to you? So fast and with the stream between us? Couldn't you cross that bridge?

SIMON   Perhaps it's no longer necessary.

GRUSHA   It's most necessary. Come over, Simon. Quick!

SIMON   Is the young lady saying that someone has come too late?

GRUSHA *looks up at him in despair, her face streaming with tears. He picks up a piece of wood and starts cutting it.*

THE SINGER   So many words are said, so many words are left unsaid.
The soldier has come. Whence he comes he
   doesn't say.
Hear what he thought but didn't say:
The battle began at dawn, grew bloody at noon.
The first fell before me, the second behind me, the
   third at my side.
I trod on the first, I abandoned the second, the
   captain sabred the third.
My one brother died by steel, my other brother
   died by smoke.
My neck was burnt by fire, my hands froze in my
   gloves, my toes in my socks.
For food I had aspen buds, for drink I had maple
   brew, for bed I had stones in water.

SIMON   I see a cap in the grass. Is there a little one already?

GRUSHA   There is, Simon. How could I hide it? But please
don't let it worry you. It's not mine.

SIMON   They say: Once the wind begins to blow, it blows
through every crack. The woman need say no more.

GRUSHA *lowers her head and says no more.*

THE SINGER   There was great yearning but there was no waiting.
The oath is broken. Why was not disclosed.
Hear what she thought, but didn't say:
While you fought in the battle, soldier
The bloody battle, the bitter battle
I found a child who was helpless
And hadn't the heart to do away with it.
I had to care for what otherwise would have come
   to harm.

I had to bend down on the floor for breadcrumbs
I had to tear myself to pieces for what was not mine
But alien.
Someone must be the helper.
Because the little tree needs its water
The little lamb loses its way when the herdsman is
    asleep
And the bleating remains unheard.

SIMON   Give me back the cross I gave you. Or better, throw
it in the stream.

He turns to go.

GRUSHA   Simon Chachava, don't go away. It isn't mine, it isn't mine!
(*She hears the children calling.*) What is it, children?

VOICES   Soldiers have come! – They are taking Michael away!

GRUSHA *stands aghast as two Ironshirts, with Michael
between them, come towards her.*

IRONSHIRT   Are you Grusha? (*She nods.*) Is that your child?

GRUSHA   Yes. (SIMON *goes off.*) Simon!

IRONSHIRT   We have official orders to take this child, found in
your charge, back to the city. There is suspicion that
it is Michael Abashvili, son and heir of the late
Governor Georgi Abashvili, and his wife, Natella
Abashvili. Here is the document and the seal.

They lead the child away.

GRUSHA   (*running after them and shouting*) Leave it here,
please! It's mine!

THE SINGER   The Ironshirts took the child away, the precious
    child.
The unhappy girl followed them to the city, the
    dangerous place.
The real mother demanded the child back. The
    foster mother faced her trial.
Who will try the case, on whom will the child be
    bestowed?
Who will be the Judge? A good one, a bad one?
The city was in flames. On the Judgment Seat sat
    Azdak.

5

The Story of the Judge

THE SINGER	Listen now to the story of the Judge:
	How he turned Judge, how he passed judgment, what kind of Judge he is.
	On the Easter Sunday of the great revolt, when the Grand Duke was overthrown
	And his Governor Abashvili, father of our child, lost his head
	The village clerk Azdak found a fugitive in the woods and hid him in his hut.

AZDAK, in rags and tipsy, helps a fugitive dressed as a beggar into his hut.

AZDAK   Don't snort. You're not a horse. And it won't do you any good with the police if you run like a dirty nose in April. Stop, I tell you. (*He catches* THE FUGITIVE, *who has trotted into the hut as though he would go through the walls.*) Sit down and feed: here's a piece of cheese. (*From under some rags in a chest he fishes out some cheese, and* THE FUGITIVE *greedily begins to eat.*) Haven't had anything for some time, eh? (THE FUGITIVE *groans.*) Why did you run so fast, you arse-hole? The police wouldn't even have seen you!

THE FUGITIVE   Had to.

AZDAK   Blue funk? (THE FUGITIVE *stares, uncomprehending.*) Got the squitters? Afraid? Don't slobber like a Grand Duke or a sow. I can't stand it. It's well-born stinkers we've got to put up with as God made them. Not the likes of you. I once heard of a Senior Judge who farted at a public dinner. Just to show his independence. Watching you eat like that really gives me the most awful ideas! Why don't you say something? (*Sharply.*) Let's have a look at your hand. Can't you hear? Show me your hand. (THE FUGITIVE *slowly puts out his hand.*) White! So you're no beggar at all! A fraud! A swindle on legs! And here am I hiding you from the police as though you were a decent human being! Why run like that if you're a landowner? Because that's what you are. Don't try to deny it. I see it in your guilty face. (*He gets up.*) Get out of here! (THE FUGITIVE *looks uncertainly at him.*) What are you waiting for, you peasant-flogger?

THE FUGITIVE Am hunted. Ask for undivided attention. Make proposition.

AZDAK What do you want to make? A proposition? Well, if that isn't the height of insolence! He making a proposition! The bitten man scratches his fingers bloody, and the leech makes a proposition. Get out, I tell you!

THE FUGITIVE Understand point of view. Persuasion. Will pay 100,000 piastres for one night. How's that?

AZDAK What? Do you think you can buy me? And for 100,000 piastres? A third-rate farm. Let's say 150,000. Got it?

THE FUGITIVE Not on me, of course. Will be sent. Hope, don't doubt.

AZDAK Doubt profoundly! Get out!

THE FUGITIVE *gets up and trots to the door. A voice from off-stage.*

VOICE Azdak!

THE FUGITIVE *turns, trots to the opposite corner and stands still.*

AZDAK (*shouting*) I'm not in. (*He walks to the door.*) Is that you spying around here again, Shauva?

POLICEMAN SHAUVA (*outside, reproachfully*) You've snared another rabbit, Azdak. You promised me it wouldn't happen again.

AZDAK (*severely*) Shauva, don't talk about things you don't understand. The rabbit is a dangerous and destructive animal. It devours plants, especially what they call weeds. So it must be exterminated.

SHAUVA Azdak, don't be so hard on me. I'll lose my job if I don't arrest you. I know you have a good heart.

AZDAK I *don't* have a good heart! How often am I to tell you I'm a man of intellect?

SHAUVA (*slyly*) I know, Azdak. You're a superior person. You

say so yourself. I'm a Christian and I've no education. So
I ask you: if one of the Prince's rabbits is stolen, and I'm
a policeman, what am I to do with the offender?

AZDAK   Shauva, Shauva, shame on you! There you stand asking
me a question. Nothing is more tempting than a
question. Suppose you were a woman – let's say
Nunovna, that bad girl – and you showed me your thigh
– Nunovna's thigh, that is – and you asked me: what
shall I do with my thigh? It itches. Is she as innocent as
she pretends? No. I catch a rabbit, you catch a man.
Man is made in God's image. Not so a rabbit, you know
that. I'm a rabbit-eater; but you're a man-eater, Shauva.
And God will pass judgment on you. Shauva, go home
and repent. No, stop! There's something … (*He looks
at* THE FUGITIVE, *who stands trembling in the corner.*)
No, it's nothing after all. Go home and repent. (*He
slams the door behind* SHAUVA. *To* THE FUGITIVE) Now
you're surprised, eh? Surprised I didn't hand you over?
But I couldn't hand over even a bedbug to that beast of
a policeman! It goes against my grain. Don't tremble at
the sight of a policeman. So old and yet so cowardly!
Finish your cheese, but eat it like a poor man, or else
they'll still catch you. Do I even have to tell you how a
poor man behaves? (*He makes him sit down, and then
gives him back the cheese.*) The box is the table. Put
your elbows on the table, and now surround the plate
with your arms as though you expected the cheese to
be snatched from you at any moment. What right have
you to be safe? Now hold the knife as if it were a small
sickle; and don't look so greedily at your cheese, look at
it mournfully – because it's already disappearing – like
all good things. (AZDAK *watches him.*) They're after you.
That speaks in your favour. But how can I be sure
they're not mistaken about you? In Tiflis they once
hanged a landowner, a Turk. He could prove he
quartered his peasants instead of merely cutting them
in half, as is the custom. And he squeezed twice the
usual amount of taxes out of them. His zeal was
above all suspicion, and yet they hanged him
like a common criminal. Why? Because he was

a Turk – something he couldn't do much about. An
injustice! He got on to the gallows like Pontius Pilate
into the Creed. In a word, I don't trust you.

THE SINGER   Thus Azdak gave shelter to the old beggar
               Only to find out that he was that Murderer, the
                    Grand Duke.
               And he was ashamed of himself, he accused
                    himself and ordered the policeman
               To take him to Nukha, to Court, to be judged.

*In the Court of Justice three Ironshirts sit drinking.
From a pillar hangs a man in judge's robes. Enter*
AZDAK, *in chains, dragging* SHAUVA *behind him.*

AZDAK   (*shouting*) I have helped the Grand Duke, the Grand
               Thief, the Grand Murderer, to escape! In the name of
               justice, I demand to be judged severely in a public trial!

THE FIRST   Who is this queer bird?
IRONSHIRT

SHAUVA   That's our clerk, Azdak.

AZDAK   I am despicable, treacherous, branded! Tell them,
               flatfoot, how I insisted on being put in chains and
               brought to the capital. Because I sheltered the Grand
               Duke, the Grand Swindler, by mistake. As I realized
               only afterwards when I found this document in my
               hut. (*The Ironshirts study the document. To* SHAUVA)
               They can't read. Point out that the branded man is
               accusing himself. Tell them how I forced you to walk
               with me through half the night, to get everything
               cleared up.

SHAUVA   And all by threats. That wasn't nice of you, Azdak.

AZDAK   Shauva, shut your trap. You don't understand. A new
               age has come, which will thunder over you. You're
               finished. The police are being wiped out, pfft!
               Eveything is being investigated, brought into the
               open. In which case a man prefers to give himself up.
               Why? Because he won't escape the mob. Tell them
               how I've been shouting all along Shoemaker Street!
               (*He acts with expansive gestures, looking sideways
               at the Ironshirts.*) 'Out of ignorance I let the

Grand Swindler escape. Tear me to pieces, brothers!'
So as to get in first.

THE FIRST
IRONSHIRT
And what was their answer?

SHAUVA
They comforted him in Butcher Street, and laughed
themselves sick in Shoemaker Street. That's all.

AZDAK
But here with you it's different, I know you're men of
iron. Brothers, where is the Judge? I must be tried.

THE FIRST
IRONSHIRT
(*pointing at the hanged man*) Here's the Judge. And
stop 'brothering' us. That's rather a sore spot this
evening.

AZDAK
'Here's the Judge.' That's an answer never heard in
Grusinia before. Citizens, where's His Excellency the
Governor? (*Pointing at the gallows*) Here's His
Excellency, stranger. Where's the Chief Tax
Collector? Where's the official Recruiting Officer?
The Patriarch? The Chief of Police? Here, here, here –
all here. Brothers, that's what I expected from you.

THE SECOND
IRONSHIRT
Stop! What did you expect, you bird?

AZDAK
What happened in Persia, brothers. What happened
there.

THE SECOND
IRONSHIRT
And what did happen in Persia?

AZDAK
Forty years ago. Everyone hanged. Viziers, tax
collectors. My grandfather, a remarkable man, saw it
all. For three whole days. Everywhere.

THE SECOND
IRONSHIRT
And who reigned after the Vizier was hanged?

AZDAK
A peasant.

THE SECOND
IRONSHIRT
And who commanded the army?

AZDAK
A soldier, soldier.

THE SECOND
IRONSHIRT
And who paid the wages?

AZDAK
A dyer. A dyer paid the wages.

THE SECOND
IRONSHIRT
Wasn't it a carpet weaver perhaps?

THE FIRST
IRONSHIRT
And why did all this happen, you Persian?

AZDAK
'Why did all this happen?' Must there be a special

reason? Why do you scratch yourself, brother? War! Too long a war! And no justice! My grandfather brought back a song that tells what it was all about. I and my friend the policeman will sing it for you. (*To* SHAUVA) And hold on to the rope, that's part of it. (*He sings, with* SHAUVA *holding the rope.*)

> Why don't our sons bleed any longer, why don't
>   our daughters weep any more?
> Why do only the calves in the slaughterhouse have
>   any blood, why only willows on Lake Urmi tears?
> The Grand King must have a new providence, the
>   peasant must relinquish his savings.
> In order to capture the roof of the world, the
>   cottage roofs have to be torn down.
> Our men are scattered in all directions, so that the
>   great ones can eat at home.
> The soldiers kill each other, the marshals salute
>   each other.
> The widow's tax money has to be fingered to see if
>   it's good, the swords break.
> The battle has been lost, but the helmets have been
>   paid for.
> Is that right? Is that right?

SHAUVA   Yes, yes, yes, yes, yes, that's right.

AZDAK   Do you want to hear the whole thing?

The first Ironshirt nods.

THE SECOND IRONSHIRT   (*to* SHAUVA) Did he teach you that song?

SHAUVA   Yes. Only my voice isn't good.

THE SECOND IRONSHIRT   No. (*To* AZDAK) Go on singing.

AZDAK   The second verse is about the peace. (*He sings*)

> The offices are jammed, the officials are working in
>   the streets.
> The rivers overflow their banks and lay waste the
>   fields.
> Those incapable of letting down their own trousers
>   rule countries.
> Those who can't count up to four devour eight courses.

	The corn farmers look round for buyers, but see only the starving.
	The weavers go home from their looms in rags.
	Is that right? Is that right?
SHAUVA	Yes, yes, yes, yes, yes, that's right.
AZDAK	That's why our sons bleed no longer, our daughters weep no more.
	That's why only the calves in the slaughterhouse have any blood.
	And the willows in the morning on Lake Urmi have any tears.
THE FIRST IRONSHIRT	(*after a pause*) Are you going to sing that song here in town?
AZDAK	Of course. What's wrong with it?
THE FIRST IRONSHIRT	Do you see the sky getting red?
	(*Turning round,* AZDAK *sees the sky reddened by fire.*) That's in the outer town. This morning when Prince Kazbeki had Governor Abashvili beheaded our carpet weavers also caught the 'Persian disease'. They asked if Prince Kazbeki isn't eating too many courses. And this afternoon they strung up the town judge. But we beat them to pulp for two plastres per weaver, you understand?
AZDAK	(*after a pause*) I understand.
	He glances shyly round and, creeping away, sits down in a corner, his head in his hands.
THE FIRST IRONSHIRT	(*to the third, after they have all had a drink*) Just wait and see what'll happen next.
	The first and second Ironshirts walk towards AZDAK *and block his exit.*
SHAUVA	I don't think he's a really bad character, gentlemen. He poaches a few chickens here and there, and perhaps an odd rabbit.
THE SECOND IRONSHIRT	(*approaching* AZDAK) You've come here to fish in troubled waters, eh?
AZDAK	(*looking up*) I don't know why I've come here.
THE SECOND IRONSHIRT	Do you happen to be in with the

carpet weavers? (AZDAK *shakes his head.*) And what
about this song?

AZDAK From my grandfather. A stupid, ignorant man.

THE SECOND IRONSHIRT Right. And what about the dyer who paid the wages?

AZDAK That was in Persia.

THE FIRST IRONSHIRT And what about denouncing yourself for not having hanged the Grand Duke with your own hands?

AZDAK Didn't I tell you that I let him escape?

SHAUVA I swear to it. He let him escape.

The Ironshirts drag AZDAK *screaming to the gallows.
Then they let him loose and burst out laughing.*
AZDAK *joins in the laughter, laughing loudest. They
then unchain him. They all start drinking. Enter* THE
FAT PRINCE *with a young man.*

THE FIRST IRONSHIRT (*to* AZDAK) There you have your new age.

More laughter.

THE FAT PRINCE And what is there to laugh about here, my friends?
Permit me a serious word. Yesterday morning the
Princes of Grusinia overthrew the Grand Duke's
war-thirsty government and did away with his
governors. Unfortunately the Grand Duke himself
escaped. In this fateful hour our carpet weavers,
these eternal troublemakers, had the audacity to
incite a rebellion and hang our universally beloved
city Judge, our dear Illa Orbeliani. Tut-tut. My friends,
we need peace, peace, peace in Grusinia. And
justice. Here I bring you my dear nephew, Bizergan
Kazbeki! He's to be the new Judge, a talented fellow.
I say: the people must decide.

THE FIRST IRONSHIRT Does this mean we elect the Judge?

THE FAT PRINCE Precisely. The people propose a talented fellow.
Confer, my friends. (*The Ironshirts confer.*) Don't
worry, little fox. The job's yours. And once we've run
the Grand Duke to earth we won't have to kiss the
rabble's arse any more.

THE IRONSHIRTS	(*to each other*) They've got the jitters because they still haven't caught the Grand Duke. – We've this clerk to thank for that. He let him get away. – They're not sure of things yet. So they say: 'My friends!' And: 'The people must decide!' – Now he even wants justice for Grusinia! – But fun's fun as long as it lasts. – We'll ask the clerk; he knows all about justice. Hey, scoundrel …
AZDAK	You mean me?
THE FIRST IRONSHIRT	(*continues*) Would you like to have the nephew as Judge?
AZDAK	You asking me? You're not really asking me that, are you?
THE SECOND IRONSHIRT	Why not? Anything for a laugh!
AZDAK	I take it you want him put to the test? Am I right? Have you a crook on hand? An experienced one? So the candidate can show how good he is?
THE THIRD IRONSHIRT	Let me see. We have the Governor's tart's two doctors down there. Let's use them.
AZDAK	Stop! That's no good! You can't take real crooks till we're sure of the Judge being appointed. He may be an ass, but he must be appointed or else the law is violated. The law is a very sensitive organ. Like the spleen. Once attacked with fists, death occurs. You can hang those two. Why not? You won't have violated the law, because no Judge was present. Judgment must always be passed with complete solemnity – because it's such rot. Suppose a Judge throws a woman into clink for having stolen a corncake for her child. And he isn't wearing his robes. Or he's scratching himself while passing sentence so that more than a third of his body is exposed – in which case he'd have to scratch his thigh – then the sentence he passes is a disgrace and the law is violated. It would be easier for a Judge's robe and a Judge's hat to pass sentence than for a man without all that paraphernalia. If you don't look out, the law goes up in smoke. You don't taste wine by offering it to a dog. Why not? Because the wine would be gone.

THE FIRST IRONSHIRT	So what do you suggest, you hair-splitter?
AZDAK	I'll be the defendant. I even know what sort. (AZDAK *whispers to them.*)
THE FIRST IRONSHIRT	You? (*All burst out laughing.*)
THE FAT PRINCE	What have you decided?
THE FIRST IRONSHIRT	We've decided to have a rehearsal. Our good friend will act as defendant, and here's the Judge's seat for the candidate.
THE FAT PRINCE	That's unusual. But why not? (*To* THE NEPHEW) A mere formality, little fox. What did they teach you? Who gets there first? The slow runner or the fast one?
THE NEPHEW	The silent one, Uncle Arsen.

THE NEPHEW *sits in the Judge's seat,* THE FAT PRINCE *standing behind him. The Ironshirts sit on the steps. Enter* AZDAK, *imitating the unmistakeable gait of the Grand Duke.*

AZDAK	Is there anyone here who knows me? I am the Grand Duke.
THE FAT PRINCE	What is he?
THE SECOND IRONSHIRT	The Grand Duke. He really does know him.
THE FAT PRINCE	Good.
THE FIRST IRONSHIRT	Get on with the proceedings.
AZDAK	Listen! I'm accused of war-mongering. Ridiculous! Am saying: ridiculous! Is that enough? If not, have brought lawyers along. About 500. (*He points behind him, pretending to be surrounded by lawyers.*) Requisition all available seats for lawyers. (*The Ironshirts laugh;* THE FAT PRINCE *joins in.*)
THE NEPHEW	(*to the Ironshirts*) Do you want me to try this case? I must admit I find it rather unusual. From the point of view of taste, I mean.
THE FIRST IRONSHIRT	Go on.
THE FAT PRINCE	(*smiling*) Let him have it, little fox!
THE NEPHEW	All right. People of Grusinia versus Grand Duke. What have you to say, defendant?
AZDAK	Any amount. Of course, have myself read war lost. Started war at the time on advice of patriots like Uncle

	Kazbeki. Demand Uncle Kazbeki as witness. (*The Ironshirts laugh.*)
THE FAT PRINCE	(*to the Ironshirts, affably*) Quite a card, eh?
THE NEPHEW	Motion overruled. You're being accused not of declaring war, which every ruler has to do once in a while, but of conducting it badly.
AZDAK	Rot! Didn't conduct it at all! Had it conducted. Had it conducted by Princes. Made a mess of it, of course.
THE NEPHEW	Do you deny having been Commander in Chief?
AZDAK	Not at all. Always was Commander in Chief. Even at birth ticked off wet-nurse; dismissed turds promptly in potty. Got used to command. Always commanded officals to rob my cash-box. Officers flog soldiers only on my command. Landlords sleep with peasant's wives only when strictly commanded by me. Uncle Kazbeki here grew stomach only on my command.
THE IRONSHIRTS	(*clapping*) He's good! Up the Grand Duke!
THE FAT PRINCE	Answer him, little fox! I'm with you!
THE NEPHEW	I shall answer him according to the dignity of the law. Defendant, preserve the dignity of the law.
AZDAK	Agreed. Command you proceed with the trial.
THE NEPHEW	It's not your business to command me. So you claim the Princes forced you to declare war. Then how can you claim they made a mess of it?
AZDAK	Didn't send enough troops. Embezzled funds. Brought sick horses. During attack found drunk in whore-house. Propose Uncle Kaz as witness. (THE IRONSHIRTS *laugh.*)
THE NEPHEW	Are you making the outragcous claim that the Princes of this country did not fight?
AZDAK	No. Princes fought. Fought for war contracts.
THE FAT PRINCE	(*jumping up*) That's too much! This man talks like a carpet weaver!
AZDAK	Really? Only telling the truth!
THE FAT PRINCE	Hang him! Hang Him!
THE FIRST IRONSHIRT	Keep quiet. Get on, Excellency.
THE NEPHEW	Quiet! Now pass sentence. Must be hanged.

Hanged by the neck. Having lost war. Sentence passed. No appeal.

THE FAT PRINCE   (*hysterically*) Away with him! Away with him! Away with him!

AZDAK   Young man, seriously advise not to fall publicly into jerky, clipped manner of speech. Can't be employed as watchdog if howl like wolf. Got it?

THE FAT PRINCE   Hang him!

AZDAK   If people realize Princes talk same language as Grand Dukes, may even hang Grand Dukes and Princes. By the way, sentence quashed. Reason: war lost, but not for Princes. Princes have won *their* war. Got themselves paid 3,863,000 piastres for horses not delivered.

THE FAT PRINCE   Hang him!

AZDAK   8,240,000 piastres for food supplies not produced.

THE FAT PRINCE   Hang him!

AZDAK   Are therefore victors. War lost only for Grusinia, which is not present in this Court.

THE FAT PRINCE   I think that's enough, my friends. (*To* AZDAK) You can withdraw, gaol-bird. (*To* THE IRONSHIRTS) I think you can now ratify the new Judge's appointment, my friends.

THE FIRST IRONSHIRT   Yes, we can do that. Take down the Judge's robe. (*One of* THE IRONSHIRTS *climbs on the back of another and pulls the robe off the hanged man.*) And now – (*to* THE NEPHEW) – you be off so that we can put the right arse on the right seat. (*To* AZDAK) Step forward, you, and sit on the Judge's seat. (AZDAK *hesitates.*) Sit down up there, man. (AZDAK *is thrust on to the seat by* THE IRONSHIRTS.) The Judge was always a rascal. Now the rascal shall be the Judge. (*The Judge's robe is placed round his shoulders, the wicker from a bottle on his head.*) Look! There's a Judge for you!

THE SINGER   Now there was civil war in the land. The rulers were unsafe.
Now Azdak was made a Judge by the Ironshirts.
Now Azdak remained a Judge for two years.

THE SINGER WITH HIS MUSICIANS

> Great houses turn to ashes
>> And blood runs down the street.
> Rats come out of the sewers
>> And maggots out of the meat.
> The thug and the blasphemer
>> Lounge by the altar-stone:
> Now, now, now Azdak
>> Sits on the Judgment throne.

AZDAK *sits on the Judge's seat peeling an apple. SHAUVA sweeps out the hall. On one side an invalid in a wheelchair, the accused doctor and a man in rags with a limp; opposite, a young man accused of blackmail.* AN IRONSHIRT *stands on guard holding* THE IRONSHIRTS' *banner.*

AZDAK In view of the large number of cases, the Court today will hear two cases simultaneously. Before I open the proceedings, a short announcement: I receive – (*he stretches out his hand; only* THE BLACKMAILER *produces some money and hands it to him*) – I reserve for myself the right to punish one of these parties here – (*he glances at* THE INVALID) – for contempt of court. You – (*to* THE DOCTOR) – are a doctor, and you – (*to* THE INVALID) – are bringing a complaint against him. Is the doctor responsible for your condition?

THE INVALID Yes. I had a stroke because of him.

AZDAK That sounds like professional negligence.

THE INVALID More than negligence. I gave this man money to study. So far he hasn't paid me back one penny. And when I heard he was treating a patient free, I had a stroke.

AZDAK Rightly. (*To* THE LIMPING MAN) And you, what do you want here?

THE LIMPING MAN I'm the patient, your Worship.

AZDAK He treated your leg?

THE LIMPING MAN Not the right one. My rheumatism was in the left leg, and he operated on my right. That's why I'm limping now.

AZDAK And you got that free?

THE INVALID   A 500-piastre operation free! For nothing! For a
                 God-Bless-You! And I paid this man's studies! (*To* THE
                 DOCTOR) Did you learn to operate for nothing at school?

THE DOCTOR   (*to* AZDAK) Your Worship, it is actually the custom to
                 demand the fee before the operation, as the patient is
                 more willing to pay before an operation than after.
                 Which is only human. In this case I was convinced,
                 when I started the operation, that my servant had
                 already received the fee. In this I was mistaken.

THE INVALID   He was mistaken! A good doctor doesn't make
                 mistakes. He examines before he operates.

AZDAK   That's right. (*To* SHAUVA) Public Prosecutor, what's the
                 other case about?

SHAUVA   (*busily sweeping*) Blackmail.

THE BLACKMAILER High Court of Justice, I'm innocent. I only wanted to
                 find out from the landowner in question if he really
                 had raped his niece. He kindly informed me that this
                 was not the case, and gave me the money only so
                 that I could let my uncle study music.

AZDAK   Ah ha! (*To* THE DOCTOR) You on the other hand can't
                 produce any extenuating circumstances in your defence?

THE DOCTOR   Except that to err is human.

AZDAK   And you know that in money matters a good doctor
                 is conscious of his responsibility? I once heard of a
                 doctor who made a thousand piastres out of one
                 sprained finger: he discovered it had something to do
                 with the circulation of the blood, which a less good
                 doctor would have overlooked. On another occasion,
                 by careful treatment, he turned a mediocre gall
                 bladder into a gold mine. You have no excuses,
                 Doctor. The corn merchant Uxu made his son study
                 medicine to get some knowledge of trade – our
                 medical schools are that good. (*To* THE BLACKMAILER)
                 What's the name of the landowner?

SHAUVA   He doesn't want it to be known.

AZDAK   In that case I will pass judgment. The Court considers
                 the blackmail proved. And you – (*to* THE INVALID) – are
                 sentenced to a fine of 1000 piastres. If you get a second

stroke the doctor will have to treat you free and if necessary amputate. (*To* THE LIMPING MAN) As compensation, you will receive a bottle of embrocation. (*To* THE BLACKMAILER) You are sentenced to hand over half the proceeds of your deal to the Public Prosecutor, to keep the landowner's name secret. You are advised, moreover, to study medicine. You seem well suited to that profession. And you, Doctor, are acquitted because of an inexcusable professional mistake. The next cases!

THE SINGER WITH HIS MUSICIANS

> Beware of willing Judges
>> For Truth is a black cat
> In a windowless room at midnight
>> And Justice a blind bat.
> A third and shrugging party
>> Alone can right our wrong.
> This, this, this, Azdak
>> Does for a mere song.

Enter AZDAK *from the caravansary on the highway, followed by the old, bearded* INNKEEPER. *The Judge's seat is carried by a manservant and* SHAUVA. *An Ironshirt with a banner takes up position.*

AZDAK   Put it here. Then at least we can get some air and a little breeze from the lemon grove over there. It's good for Justice to do it in the open. The wind blows her skirts up and you see what's underneath. Shauva, we have eaten too much. These rounds of inspection are very exhausting. (*To* THE INNKEEPER) So it's about your daughter-in-law?

THE INNKEEPER   Your Worship, it's about the family honour. I wish to bring an action on behalf of my son, who's gone on business across the mountain. This is the offending stableman, and here's my unfortunate daughter-in-law.

Enter THE DAUGHTER-IN-LAW, *a voluptuous wench. She is veiled.*

AZDAK   (*sitting down*) I receive. (*Sighing,* THE INNKEEPER *hands him some money.*) Good. Now the formalities are disposed of. This is a case of rape?

THE INNKEEPER   Your Worship, I surprised this rascal in the stable in the act of laying our Ludovica in the straw.

AZDAK	Quite right, the stable. Beautiful horses. I particularly like the little roan.
THE INNKEEPER	The first thing I did of course was to berate Ludovica on behalf of my son.
AZDAK	(*seriously*) I said I liked the little roan.
THE INNKEEPER	(*coldly*) Really? – Ludovica admitted that the stableman took her against her will.
AZDAK	Take off your veil, Ludovica. (*She does so.*) Ludovica, you please the Court. Tell us how it happened.
LUDOVICA	(*as though well rehearsed*) When I entered the stable to look at the new foal, the stableman said to me of his own accord: 'It's hot today' and laid his hand on my left breast. I said to him: 'Don't do that!' But he continued to handle me indecently, which provoked my anger. Before I realized his sinful intentions, he became intimate with me. It had already happened when my father-in-law entered and accidentally trod on me.
THE INNKEEPER	(*explaining*) On behalf of my son.
AZDAK	(*to* THE STABLEMAN) Do you admit that you started it?
THE STABLEMAN	Yes
AZDAK	Ludovica, do you like to eat sweet things?
LUDOVICA	Yes, sunflower seeds.
AZDAK	Do you like sitting a long time in the tub?
LUDOVICA	Half an hour or so.
AZDAK	Public Prosecutor, just drop your knife on the floor. (SHAUVA *does so.*) Ludovica, go and pick up the Public Prosecutor's knife.

LUDOVICA, *hips swaying, goes and picks up the knife.*
(AZDAK *points at her.*) Do you see that? The way it sways? The criminal element has been discovered. The rape has been proved. By eating too much, especially sweet things, by lying too long in warm water, by laziness and too soft a skin, you have raped the poor man. Do you imagine you can go around with a bottom like that and get away with it in Court? This is a case of deliberate assault with a dangerous weapon. You are sentenced to hand over to the Court the little roan which your father liked to ride on behalf of

his son. And now, Ludovica, come with me to the stable so that the Court may investigate the scene of the crime.

AZDAK *is carried on his Judge's seat by Ironshirts from place to place on the Grusinian highway. Behind him come* SHAUVA *dragging the gallows and* THE STABLEMAN *leading the little roan.*

THE SINGER WITH HIS MUSICIANS

No more did the Lower Orders
  Tremble in their shoes
At the bellows of their Betters
  At *Come-Here's* and *Listen-You's.*
His balances were crooked
  But they shouted in the streets:—
  'Good, good, good is Azdak
  And the measure that he metes!'

He took them from Wealthy Peter
  To give to Penniless Paul
Sealed his illegal judgments
  With a waxen tear, and all
The rag-tag-and-bobtail
  Ran crying up and down:—
  'Cheer, cheer, cheer for Azdak
  The darling of the town!'

The little group slowly withdraws.

To love your next-door neighbour
  Approach him with an axe
For prayers and saws and sermons
  Are unconvincing facts.
What miracles of preaching
  A good sharp blade can do:
So, so, so, so Azdak
  Makes miracles come true.

AZDAK's *Judge's seat is in a tavern. Three farmers stand before* AZDAK. SHAUVA *brings him wine. In a corner stands an old peasant woman. In the open doorway, and outside, stand villagers and spectators. An Ironshirt stands guard with a banner.*

AZDAK	The Public Prosecutor opens the proceedings.
SHAUVA	It's about a cow. For five weeks the defendant has had a cow in her stable, the property of farmer Suru. She was also found to be in the possession of a stolen ham. And cows belonging to farmer Shutoff were killed after he had asked the defendant to pay the rent for a field.
THE FARMERS	It's about my ham, Your Worship. – It's about my cow, Your Worship. – It's about my field, Your Worship.
AZDAK	Granny, what have you got to say to all this?
THE OLD WOMAN	Your Worship, one night towards morning, five weeks ago, there was a knock at my door, and outside stood a bearded man with a cow. He said, 'Dear woman, I am the miracle-working St Banditus. And because your son has been killed in the war, I bring you this cow as a keepsake. Take good care of it!'
THE FARMERS	The robber Irakli, Your Worship! – Her brother-in-law, Your Worship! The cattle thief, the incendiary! – He must be beheaded!

Outside a woman screams. The crowd grows restless and retreats. Enter THE BANDIT *Irakli, with a huge axe.*

THE FARMERS	Irakli! (*They cross themselves.*)
THE BANDIT	A very good evening, dear friends! A glass of wine!
AZDAK	Public Prosecutor, a jug of wine for the guest. And who are you?
THE BANDIT	I'm a wandering hermit, Your Worship. And thank you for the kind gift. (*He empties the glass which* SHAUVA *has brought.*) Same again!
AZDAK	I'm Azdak. (*He gets up and bows.* THE BANDIT *also bows.*) The Court welcomes the stranger hermit. Go on with your story, Granny.
THE OLD WOMAN	Your Worship, that first night I didn't know that St Banditus could work miracles, it was only the cow. But one night a few days later the farmer's servants came to take the cow away from me. Then they turned round in front of my door and went off without the cow.

And on their heads sprouted bumps big as a fist.
Then I knew that St Banditus had changed their
hearts and turned them into friendly people.

THE BANDIT *roars with laughter.*

THE FIRST FARMER   I know what changed them.

AZDAK   That's good. You can tell us later. Continue.

THE OLD WOMAN   Your Worship, the next one to become a good man
was farmer Shutoff – a devil, as everyone knows. But
St Banditus brought it about that Shutoff let me off
paying the rent for the field.

THE SECOND FARMER   Because my cows were killed in the field.

THE BANDIT *laughs.*

THE OLD WOMAN   (*answering* AZDAK*'s sign to continue*) And then one
morning the ham came flying in at my window. It hit
me in the small of the back. I've been lame ever
since. Look, Your Worship. (*She limps a few steps.*
THE BANDIT *laughs.*) I ask Your Worship: when was a
poor old body ever given a ham except by a miracle?

THE BANDIT *starts sobbing.*

AZDAK   (*rising from his seat*) Granny, that's a question that
strikes straight at the Court's heart. Be so kind as to
sit down here.

Hesitating, THE OLD WOMAN *sits on the Judge's seat.*
AZDAK *sits on the floor, glass in hand.*

Little mother, I almost called you Mother Grusinia,
the woebegone.
The bereaved one, whose sons are in the war.
Who is beaten with fists, but full of hope.
Who weeps when she is given a cow
And is surprised when she is not beaten.
Little mother, pass merciful sentence on us, the damned!
He bellows to the farmers.

Admit that you don't believe in miracles, you
atheists! Each of you is sentenced to pay 500 piastres!
For your lack of faith. Get out!

The farmers creep out.

And you, little mother, and you – (*to* THE BANDIT) –
pious man, drink a jug of wine with the Public
Prosecutor and Azdak!

THE SINGER WITH HIS MUSICIANS

> To feed the starving people
>   He broke the laws like bread
> There on the seat of justice
>   With the gallows over his head
> For more than seven hundred
>   Days he calmed their wails
> Well, well, well, did Azdak
>   Measure with false scales.
> Two summers and two winters
>   A poor man judged the poor
> And on the wreck of justice
>   He brought them safe to shore
> For he spoke in the mob language
>   That the mob understands.
> I, I, I, cried Azdak
>   Take bribes from empty hands.

THE SINGER   Then the era of disorder was over, the Grand Duke
                  returned.
                  The Governor's wife returned, a Judgment was
                  held.
                  Many people died, the suburbs burned anew, and
                  fear seized Azdak.

AZDAK'*s Judge's seat stands again in the Court of
Justice.* AZDAK *sits on the ground mending a shoe
and talking to* SHAUVA. *Noises outside. Above a wall*
THE FAT PRINCE'*s head is carried by on a lance.*

AZDAK   Shauva, your days of slavery are numbered, perhaps
                 even the minutes. For a long time I have held you on
                 the iron curb of reason, and it has made your mouth
                 bloody. I have lashed you with arguments founded
                 on reason, and ill-treated you with logic. You are
                 by nature a weak creature, and if one slyly throws
                 you an argument, you have to devour it; you can't
                 resist. By nature you are compelled to lick the
                 hand of a superior being, but superior beings

can be very different. And now comes your liberation, and you will soon be able to follow your inclinations, which are low. You will be able to follow your unerring instinct, which teaches you to plant your heavy boot on the faces of men. Gone is the era of confusion and disorder, and the great times which I found described in the Song of Chaos have not yet come. Let us now sing that song together in memory of those wonderful days. Sit down and don't violate the music. Don't be afraid. It sounds all right. It has a popular refrain.

(He sings)

    Sister, hide your face; brother, take your knife, the
        times are out of joint.
    The noblemen are full of complaints, the simple
        folk full of joy.
    The city says: let us drive the strong ones out of our
        midst.
    Storm the government buildings, destroy the lists
        of the serfs.
    Now the masters' noses are put to the grindstone.
        Those who never saw the day have emerged.
    The poor-boxes of ebony are broken, the precious
        sesame wood is used for beds.
    He who lacked bread now possesses barns; he who lived
        on the corn of charity, now measures it out himself.

SHAUVA   Oh, oh, oh, oh.

AZDAK   Where are you, General? Please, please, please,
        please, restore order.
    The son of the nobleman can no longer be
        recognized; the child of the mistress becomes the
        son of her slave.
    The councillors are taking shelter in the barn; he
        who was barely allowed to sleep on the wall now
        lolls in bed.
    He who once rowed a boat now owns ships; when
        their owner looks for them, they are no longer his.
    Five men are sent out by their master. They say: go
        yourself, we have arrived.

SHAUVA   Oh, oh, oh, oh.

AZDAK   Where are you, General? Please, please, please restore order!

Yes, so it might have been, if order had been much longer neglected. But now the Grand Duke, whose life I saved like a fool, has returned to the Capital. And the Persians have lent him an army to restore order. The outer town is already in flames. Go and get me the Big Book I like to sit on. (SHAUVA *brings the book from the Judge's seat.* AZDAK *opens it.*) This is the Statute Book and I've always used it, as you can confirm.

SHAUVA   Yes, to sit on.

AZDAK   Now I'd better look and see what they can do to me, because I've always allowed the have-nots to get away with everything. And I'll have to pay for it dearly. I helped to put Poverty on to its rickety legs, so they'll hang me for drunkenness. I peeped into the rich man's pocket, which is considered bad taste. And I can't hide anywhere, for all the world knows me, since I have helped the world.

SHAUVA   Someone's coming!

AZDAK   (*in a panic walks trembling to the seat*) The game is up! But I'll give no man the pleasure of seeing human greatness. I'll beg on my knees for mercy. Spittle will slobber down my chin. The fear of death is upon me.

Enter NATELLA ABASHVILI, THE GOVERNOR'S WIFE, *followed by* THE ADJUTANT *and an Ironshirt.*

THE GOVERNOR'S WIFE   What kind of man is that, Shalva?

AZDAK   A willing one, Your Excellency, a man ready to oblige.

THE ADJUTANT   Natella Abashvili, wife of the late Governor, has just returned and is looking for her three-year-old son, Michael. She has been informed that the child was abducted to the mountains by a former servant.

AZDAK   It will be brought back, Your Highness, at your service.

THE ADJUTANT   They say that the person in question is passing it off as her own child.

AZDAK	She will be beheaded, Your Highness, at your service.
THE ADJUTANT	That's all.
THE GOVERNOR'S WIFE	(*leaving*) I don't like that man.
AZDAK	(*following her to the door, and bowing*) Everything will be arranged, Your Highness, at your service.

6
The Chalk Circle

| THE SINGER | Now listen to the story of the trial concerning the child of the Governor Abashvili To establish the true mother By the famous test of the Chalk Circle. |

The courtyard of the lawcourts in Nukha. Ironshirts lead Michael in, then go across the stage and out at the back. One Ironshirt holds GRUSHA *back under the doorway with his lance until the child has been taken away. Then she is admitted. She is accompanied by the former Governor's cook. Distant noises and a fire-red sky.*

GRUSHA	He's so good, he can wash himself already.
THE COOK	You're lucky. This is not a real Judge; this is Azdak. He's drunk and doesn't understand anything. And the biggest thieves have been acquitted by him, because he mixes everything up and because the rich never offer him big enough bribes. The likes of us get off lightly sometimes.
GRUSHA	I need some luck today.
THE COOK	Touch wood. (*She crosses herself.*) I think I'd better say a quick prayer that the Judge will be drunk.

Her lips move in prayer, while GRUSHA *looks round in vain for the child.*

| THE COOK | What I can't understand is why you want to hold on to it at any price, if it's not yours. In these days. |
| GRUSHA | It's mine, I've brought it up. |

THE COOK	But didn't you ever wonder what would happen when she returned?
GRUSHA	At first I thought I'd give it back to her. Then I thought she wouldn't return.
THE COOK	And a borrowed coat keeps one warm, too, eh? (GRUSHA *nods.*) I'll swear anything you like, because you're a decent person. (*Memorizes aloud*) I had him in my care for five piastres, and on Thursday evening, when the riots started, Grusha came to fetch him. (*She sees the soldier, Chachava, approaching.*) But you have done Simon great wrong. I've talked to him. He can't understand it.
GRUSHA	(*unaware of* SIMON*'s presence*) I can't be bothered with that man just now, if he doesn't understand anything.
THE COOK	He has understood that the child is not yours; but that you're married and won't be free until death parts you – he can't understand that.

GRUSHA *sees* SIMON *and greets him.*

SIMON	(*gloomily*) I wanted to tell the woman that I am ready to swear I am the father of the child.
GRUSHA	(*low*) That's right, Simon.
SIMON	At the same time, I would like to say that I am hereby not bound to anything; nor the woman, either.
THE COOK	That's unnecessary. She's married. You know that.
SIMON	That's her business and doesn't need rubbing in.

Enter two IRONSHIRTS.

THE IRONSHIRTS	Where's the Judge? – Has anyone seen the Judge?
GRUSHA	(*who has turned away and covered her face*) Stand in front of me. I shouldn't have come to Nukha. If I run into the Ironshirt, the one I hit over the head …

THE IRONSHIRT *who has brought in the child steps forward.*

THE IRONSHIRT	The Judge isn't here.

THE TWO IRONSHIRTS *go on searching.*

THE COOK	I hope something hasn't happened to him. With any other Judge you'd have less chance than a chicken has teeth.

Enter another IRONSHIRT.

THE IRONSHIRT	(*who had inquired for the Judge, to the other* IRONSHIRT.) There are only two old people and a child here. The Judge has bolted.
THE OTHER IRONSHIRT	Go on searching!

The first two IRONSHIRTS *exit quickly. The third remains behind.* GRUSHA *lets out a scream.* THE IRONSHIRT *turns round. He is* THE CORPORAL, *and has a large scar right across his face.*

THE IRONSHIRT	(*in the gateway*) What's the matter, Shotta? Do you know her?
THE CORPORAL	(*after a long stare*) No.
THE IRONSHIRT	She's the one who's supposed to have stolen the Abashvili child. If you know anything about it, Shotta, you can make a packet of money.

Exit THE CORPORAL, *cursing.*

THE COOK	Was it him? (GRUSHA *nods.*) I think he'll keep his mouth shut, otherwise he'll have to admit he was after the child.
GRUSHA	(*relieved*) I'd almost forgotten I'd saved the child from them ...

Enter THE GOVERNOR'S WIFE, *followed by* THE ADJUTANT *and* TWO LAWYERS.

THE GOVERNOR'S WIFE	Thank God! At least the common people aren't here. I can't stand their smell, it always gives me migraine.
THE FIRST LAWYER	Madam, I must ask you to be as careful as possible in everything you say, until we have another Judge.
THE GOVERNOR'S WIFE	But I didn't say anything, Illo Shuboladze. I love the people – with their simple, straightforward ways. It's just their smell that brings on my migraine.
THE SECOND LAWYER	There will hardly be any spectators. Most of the population is behind locked doors because of the riots in the outer town.
THE GOVERNOR'S WIFE	(*looking at* GRUSHA) Is that the creature?
THE FIRST LAWYER	I beg you, most gracious Natella

Abashvili, to abstain from all invective until it is absolutely certain that the Grand Duke has appointed a new Judge and we have got rid of the present one, who is about the lowest ever seen in a Judge's robe. And things seem to be on the move, as you will see.

IRONSHIRTS *enter the courtyard.*

THE COOK Her Ladyship wouldn't hesitate to pull your hair out if she didn't know that Azdak is for the poor people. He goes by the face.

Two IRONSHIRTS *begin by fastening a rope to the pillar.* AZDAK, *in chains, is led in, followed by* SHAUVA, *also in chains. The three farmers bring up the rear.*

ONE IRONSHIRT Trying to run away, eh? (*He beats* AZDAK.)

ONE FARMER Pull the Judge's robe off before we string him up!

IRONSHIRTS *and* FARMERS *pull the robe off* AZDAK. *His torn underwear becomes visible. Then someone kicks him.*

AN IRONSHIRT (*pushing him on to someone else.*) Anyone want a bundle of Justice? Here it is!

Accompanied by shouts of 'It's all yours!' and 'I don't want it!' they hurl AZDAK *back and forth until he collapses. Then he is hauled up and dragged under the noose.*

THE GOVERNOR'S WIFE (*who, during the 'ball-game', has been clapping her hands hysterically*) I disliked that man from the moment I first saw him.

AZDAK (*covered in blood, panting*) I can't see. Give me a rag.

THE OTHER IRONSHIRT What is it you want to see?

AZDAK You, you dogs! (*He wipes the blood out of his eyes with his shirt.*) Good morning, dogs! How are you, dogs? How's the dog world? Does it stink good? Have you got another boot to lick? Are you back at each other's throats, dogs?

Enter a dust-covered RIDER *accompanied by a corporal. He takes some documents from a leather case and looks through them. He interrupts.*

THE RIDER Stop! I bring a despatch from the Grand Duke, containing the latest appointments.

THE CORPORAL	(*bellows*) Atten - shun!
	All jump to attention.
THE RIDER	Of the new Judge it says: We appoint a man whom we have to thank for the saving of a life of the utmost importance to the country. A certain Azdak in Nukha. Which is he?
SHAUVA	(*pointing*) That's him on the gallows, Your Excellency.
THE CORPORAL	(*bellowing*) What's going on here?
THE IRONSHIRT	I ask to be allowed to report that His Worship has already been His Worship. He was declared the enemy of the Grand Duke only on these farmers' denunciation.
THE CORPORAL	(*pointing at* THE FARMERS) March them off! (*They are marched off, bowing incessantly.*) See to it that His Worship is exposed to no more indignities.
	Exit the rider with THE CORPORAL.
THE COOK	(*to* SHAUVA) She clapped her hands! I hope he saw it!
THE FIRST LAWYER	This is a catastrophe.
	AZDAK *has fainted. Coming to, he is dressed again in a Judge's robe. He walks away, swaying, from the group of* IRONSHIRTS.
THE IRONSHIRTS	Don't take it amiss, Your Worship. What are Your Worship's wishes?
AZDAK	Nothing, fellow dogs. An occasional boot to lick. (*To* SHAUVA) I pardon you. (*He is unchained.*) Fetch me some of the red wine. The sweetest. (*Exit* SHAUVA.) Get out of here, I've got to judge a case. (THE IRONSHIRTS *go.* SHAUVA *returns with a jug of wine.* AZDAK *takes deep gulps.*) Get me something for my backside. (SHAUVA *brings the Statute Book and puts it on the Judge's seat.* AZDAK *sits on it.*) I receive! (*The faces of the prosecutors, among whom a worried council has been held, show smiles of relief. They whisper.*)
THE COOK	Oh dear!
SIMON	'A well can't be filled with dew!' they say.
THE LAWYERS	(*approaching* AZDAK, *who stands up expectantly*) An absolutely ridiculous case, Your Worship. The accused has abducted the child and refuses to hand it over.

AZDAK   (*stretching out his hand, and glancing at* GRUSHA) A
         most attractive person. (*He receives more money.*) I
         open the proceedings and demand the absolute
         truth. (*To* GRUSHA) Especially from you.

THE FIRST LAWYER   High Court of Justice! Blood, as the saying goes, is
         thicker than water. This old proverb ...

AZDAK   The Court wants to know the lawyer's fee.

THE FIRST LAWYER   (*surprised*) I beg your pardon? (AZDAK *rubs his
         thumb and index finger.*) Oh, I see. 500 piastres,
         Your Worship, is the answer to the Court's
         somewhat unusual question.

AZDAK   Did you hear? The question is unusual. I ask it
         because I listen to you in a quite different way if I
         know you are good.

THE FIRST LAWYER   (*bowing*) Thank you, Your Worship. High Court of
         Justice! Of all bonds the bonds of blood are the
         strongest. Mother and child – is there a more
         intimate relationship? Can one tear a child from its
         mother? High Court of Justice! She has conceived it
         in the holy ecstasies of love. She has carried it in her
         womb. She has fed it with her blood. She has borne it
         with pain. High Court of Justice! It has been
         observed, Your Worship, how even the wild tigress,
         robbed of her young, roams restless through the
         mountains, reduced to a shadow. Nature herself ...

AZDAK   (*interrupting, to* GRUSHA) What's your answer to all
         this and anything else the lawyer might have to say?

GRUSHA   He's mine.

AZDAK   Is that all? I hope you can prove it. In any case, I advise you
         to tell me why you think the child should be given to you.

GRUSHA   I've brought him up according to my best knowledge
         and conscience. I always found him something to
         eat. Most of the time he had a roof over his head. And
         I went to all sorts of trouble for him. I had
         expenses, too. I didn't think of my own comfort.
         I brought up the child to be friendly
         with everyone. And from the beginning I taught

him to work as well as he could. But he's still very small.

THE FIRST LAWYER   Your Worship, it is significant that the person herself doesn't claim any bond of blood between herself and this child.

AZDAK   The Court takes note.

THE FIRST LAWYER   Thank you, Your Worship. Please permit a woman who has suffered much – who has already lost her husband and now also has to fear the loss of her child – to address a few words to you. Her Highness, Natella Abashvili …

THE GOVERNOR'S WIFE   (*quietly*) A most cruel fate, sir, forces me to ask you to return my beloved child. It's not for me to describe to you the tortures of a bereaved mother's soul, the anxiety, the sleepless nights, the …

THE SECOND LAWYER   (*exploding*) It's outrageous the way this woman is treated. She's not allowed to enter her husband's palace. The revenue of her estate is blocked. She is told cold-bloodedly that it's tied to the heir. She can't do anything without the child. She can't even pay her lawyers. (*To the first lawyer who, desperate about this outburst, makes frantic gestures to stop him speaking*) Dear Illo Shuboladze, why shouldn't it be divulged now that it's the Abashvili estates that are at stake?

THE FIRST LAWYER   Please, Honoured Sandro Oboladze! We had agreed … (*To* AZDAK) Of course it is correct that the trial will also decide whether our noble client will obtain the right to dispose of the large Abashvili estates. I say 'also' on purpose, because in the foreground stands the human tragedy of a mother, as Natella Abashvili has rightly explained at the beginning of her moving statement. Even if Michael Abashvili were *not* the heir to the estates, he would still be the dearly beloved child of my client.

AZDAK   Stop! The Court is touched by the mention of the estates. It's a proof of human feeling.

THE SECOND LAWYER   Thanks, Your Worship. Dear Illo Shuboladze, in any case we can prove that the person who took possession of the child is not the child's mother. Permit me to lay before the Court the bare facts. By an unfortunate chain of circumstances, the child, Michael Abashvili, was left behind while his mother was making her escape. Grusha, the Palace kitchenmaid, was present on this Easter Sunday and was observed busying herself with the child ...

THE COOK All her mistress was thinking about was what kind of dresses she would take along.

THE SECOND LAWYER (*unmoved*) Almost a year later Grusha turned up in a mountain village with a child, and there entered into matrimony with ...

AZDAK How did you get into that mountain village?

GRUSHA On foot, Your Worship. And he was mine.

SIMON I am the father, Your Worship.

THE COOK I had him in my care for five piastres, Your Worship.

THE SECOND LAWYER This man is engaged to Grusha, High Court of Justice, and for this reason his testimony is not reliable.

AZDAK Are you the man she married in the mountain village?

SIMON No, Your Worship, she married a peasant.

AZDAK (*winking at* GRUSHA) Why? (*Pointing at* SIMON) Isn't he any good in bed? Tell the truth.

GRUSHA We didn't get that far. I married because of the child, so that he should have a roof over his head. (*Pointing at* SIMON.) He was in the war, Your Worship.

AZDAK And now he wants you again, eh?

SIMON I want to state in evidence ...

GRUSHA (*angrily*) I am no longer free, Your Worship.

AZDAK And the child, you claim, is the result of whoring? (GRUSHA *does not answer*.) I'm going to ask you a question: What kind of child is it? Is it one of those ragged street urchins? Or is it a child from a well-to-do family?

GRUSHA (*angrily*) It's an ordinary child.

AZDAK I mean, did he have fine features from the beginning?

GRUSHA   He had a nose in his face.

AZDAK   He had a nose in his face. I consider that answer of yours to be important. They say of me that once, before passing judgment, I went out and sniffed at a rosebush. Tricks of this kind are necessary nowadays. I'll cut things short now, and listen no longer to your lies. (*To* GRUSHA) Especially yours. (*To the group of defendants*) I can imagine what you've cooked up between you to cheat me. I know you. You're swindlers.

GRUSHA   (*suddenly*) I can quite understand your wanting to cut it short, having seen what you received!

AZDAK   Shut up! Did I receive anything from you?

GRUSHA   (*while* THE COOK *tries to restrain her*) Because I haven't got anything.

AZDAK   Quite true. I never get a thing from starvelings. I might just as well starve myself. You want justice, but do you want to pay for it? When you go to the butcher you know you have to pay. But to the Judge you go as though to a funeral supper.

SIMON   (*loudly*) 'When the horse was shod, the horsefly stretched out its leg', as the saying is.

AZDAK   (*eagerly accepting the challenge*) 'Better a treasure in the sewer than a stone in the mountain stream.'

SIMON   '"A fine day. Let's go fishing," said the angler to the worm.'

AZDAK   '"I'm my own master," said the servant, and cut off his foot.'

SIMON   '"I love you like a father," said the Czar to the peasant, and had the Czarevitch's head chopped off.'

AZDAK   'The fool's worst enemy is himself.'

SIMON   But 'a fart has no nose'.

AZDAK   Fined ten piastres for indecent language in Court. That'll teach you what justice is.

GRUSHA   That's a fine kind of justice. You jump on us because we don't talk so refined as that lot with their lawyers.

AZDAK   Exactly. The likes of you are too stupid. It's only right that you should get it in the neck.

GRUSHA   Because you want to pass the child on to her. She who is
too refined even to know how to change its nappies! You
don't know any more about Justice than I do, that's clear.

AZDAK   There's something in that. I'm an ignorant man. I
haven't even a decent pair of trousers under my
robe. See for yourself. With me, everything goes on
food and drink. I was educated in a convent school.
Come to think of it, I'll fine you ten piastres, too. For
contempt of Court. What's more, you're a very silly
girl to turn me against you, instead of making eyes at
me and wagging your backside a bit to keep me in a
good temper. Twenty piastres!

GRUSHA   Even if it were thirty, I'd tell you what I think of your
justice, you drunken onion! How dare you talk to me as
though you were the cracked Isaiah on the church
window! When they pulled you out of your mother, it
wasn't planned that you'd rap her over the knuckles for
pinching a little bowl of corn from somewhere! Aren't
you ashamed of yourself when you see how afraid I am
of you? But you've let yourself become their servant. So
that their houses are not taken away, because they've
stolen them. Since when do houses belong to bed-bugs?
But you're on the look-out, otherwise they couldn't
drag our men into their wars. You bribe-taker!

AZDAK *gets up. He begins to beam. With a little
hammer he knocks on the table half-heartedly as if
to get silence. But as* GRUSHA*'s scolding continues, he
only beats time with it.*
I've no respect for you. No more than for a thief or a
murderer with a knife, who does what he wants. You
can take the child away from me, a hundred against
one, but I tell you one thing: for a profession like yours,
they ought to choose only bloodsuckers and men who
rape children. As a punishment. To make them sit in
judgment over their fellow men, which is worse than
swinging from the gallows.

AZDAK   (*sitting down*) Now it will be thirty! And I won't go on
brawling with you as though we were in a tavern. What
would happen to my dignity as a Judge? I've lost all interest

in your case. Where's the couple who wanted a
divorce? (*To* SHAUVA) Bring them in. This case is
adjourned for fifteen minutes.

THE FIRST LAWYER (*to* THE GOVERNOR'S WIFE) Without producing any more
evidence, Madam, we have the verdict in the bag.

THE COOK (*to* GRUSHA) You've gone and spoiled your chances
with him. You won't get the child now.

Enter a very old couple.

THE GOVERNOR'S
WIFE Shalva, my smelling salts!

AZDAK I receive. (THE OLD COUPLE *do not understand.*) I hear
you want to be divorced. How long have you been
living together?

THE OLD WOMAN Forty years, Your Worship.

AZDAK And why d'you want a divorce?

THE OLD MAN We don't like each other, Your Worship.

AZDAK Since when?

THE OLD WOMAN Oh, from the very beginning, Your Worship.

AZDAK I'll consider your case and deliver my verdict when
I'm finished with the other one. (SHAUVA *leads them
into the background.*) I need the child. (*He beckons*
GRUSHA *towards him and bends not unkindly towards
her.*) I've noticed that you have a soft spot for justice. I
don't believe he's your child, but if he were yours,
woman, wouldn't you want him to be rich? You'd only
have to say he isn't yours and at once he'd have a
palace, scores of horses in his stable, scores of beggars
on his doorstep, scores of soldiers in his service, and
scores of petitioners in his courtyard. Now, what d'you
say? Don't you want him to be rich? (GRUSHA *is silent.*)

THE SINGER Listen now to what the angry girl thought, but didn't
say. (*He sings*)

> He who wears the shoes of gold
> Tramples on the weak and old
> Does evil all day long
> And mocks at wrong.

O to carry as one's own
Heavy is the heart of stone.
The power to do ill
Wears out the will.

Hunger he will dread
Not those who go unfed:
Fear the fall of night
But not the light.

AZDAK   I think I understand you, woman.

GRUSHA   I won't give him away. I've brought him up, and he knows me.

Enter SHAUVA *with the child.*

THE GOVERNOR'S WIFE   It's in rags!

GRUSHA   That's not true. I wasn't given the time to put on his good shirt.

THE GOVERNOR'S WIFE   It's been in a pig-sty.

GRUSHA   (*furious*) I'm no pig, but there are others who are. Where did you leave your child?

THE GOVERNOR'S WIFE   I'll let you have it, you vulgar person. (*She is about to throw herself on* GRUSHA, *but is restrained by her lawyers.*) She's a criminal! She must be flogged! Right away!

THE SECOND LAWYER   (*holding his hand over her mouth*) Most gracious Natella Abashvili, you promised … Your Worship the plaintiff's nerves …

AZDAK   Plaintiff and defendant! The Court has listened to your case, and has come to no decision as to who the real mother of this child is. I as Judge have the duty of choosing a mother for the child. I'll make a test. Shauva, get a piece of chalk and draw a circle on the floor. (SHAUVA *does so.*) Now place the child in the centre. (SHAUVA *puts Michael, who smiles at* GRUSHA, *in the centre of the circle.*) Plaintiff and defendant, stand near the circle, both of you. (THE GOVERNOR'S WIFE *and* GRUSHA *step up to the circle.*) Now each of you take the child by a hand. The true mother is she who has the strength to pull the child out of the circle, towards herself.

THE SECOND LAWYER	(*quickly*) High Court of Justice, I protest! I object that the fate of the great Abashvili estates, which are bound up with the child as the heir, should be made dependent on such a doubtful wrestling match. Moreover, my client does not command the same physical strength as this person, who is accustomed to physical work.
AZDAK	She looks pretty well fed to me. Pull!

THE GOVERNOR'S WIFE *pulls the child out of the circle to her side.* GRUSHA *has let it go and stands aghast.*

THE FIRST LAWYER	(*congratulating* THE GOVERNOR'S WIFE) What did I say! The bonds of blood!
AZDAK	(*to* GRUSHA) What's the matter with you? You didn't pull!
GRUSHA	I didn't hold on to him. (*She runs to* AZDAK.) Your Worship, I take back everything I said against you. I ask your forgiveness. If I could just keep him until he can speak properly. He knows only a few words.
AZDAK	Don't influence the Court! I bet you know only twenty yourself. All right, I'll do the test once more, to make certain.

The two women take up positions again.

AZDAK	Pull!

Again GRUSHA *lets go of the child.*

GRUSHA	(*in despair*) I've brought him up! Am I to tear him to pieces? I can't do it!
AZDAK	(*rising*) And in this manner the Court has established the true mother. (*To* GRUSHA) Take your child and be off with it. I advise you not to stay in town with him. (*To* THE GOVERNOR'S WIFE) And you disappear before I fine you for fraud. Your estates fall to the city. A playground for children will be made out of them. They need one, and I have decided it shall be called after me – The Garden of Azdak.

THE GOVERNOR'S WIFE *has fainted and is carried out by* THE ADJUTANT. *Her lawyers have preceded her.* GRUSHA *stands motionless.* SHAUVA *leads the child towards her.*

AZDAK	Now I'll take off this Judge's robe – it has become

too hot for me. I'm not cut out for a hero. But I invite you all to a little farewell dance, outside on the meadow. Oh, I had almost forgotten something in the excitement. I haven't signed the decree for divorce.

Using the Judge's seat as a table, he writes something on a piece of paper and prepares to leave. Dance music has started.

SHAUVA   (*having read what is on the paper*) But that's not right. You haven't divorced the old couple. You've divorced Grusha from her husband.

AZDAK   Have I divorced the wrong ones? I'm sorry, but it'll have to stand. I never retract anything. If I did, there'd be no law and order. (*To* THE OLD COUPLE) Instead, I'll invite you to my feast. You won't mind dancing with each other. (*To* GRUSHA *and* SIMON) I've still got 40 piastres coming from you.

SIMON   (*pulling out his purse*) That's cheap. Your Worship. And many thanks.

AZDAK   (*pocketing the money*) I'll need it.

GRUSHA   So we'd better leave town tonight, eh, Michael? (*About to take the child on her back. To* SIMON) You like him?

SIMON   (*taking the child on his back*) With my respects, I like him.

GRUSHA   And now I can tell you: I took him because on that Easter Sunday I got engaged to you. And so it is a child of love. Michael, let's dance.

She dances with Michael. SIMON *dances with* THE COOK. *The* OLD COUPLE *dance with each other.* AZDAK *stands lost in thought. The dancers soon hide him from view. Occasionally he is seen again, but less and less as more couples enter and join the dance.*

THE SINGER   And after this evening Azdak disappeared and was never seen again.

But the people of Grusinia did not forget him and often remembered

His time of Judgment as a brief

Golden Age that was almost just.

The dancing couples dance out. AZDAK *has disappeared.*

But you who have listened to the story of the Chalk
  Circle
Take note of the meaning of the ancient song:
That what there is shall belong to those who are
  good for it, thus
The children to the maternal, that they thrive;
The carriages to good drivers, that they are driven
  well;
And the valley to the waterers, that they shall bear
  fruit.

QUESTIONS AND EXPLORATIONS

1 Keeping Track

A series of questions to help students articulate their response to the text during a first reading. These responses may be in the form of classroom discussion or a written reading 'journal'.

Scene One The Struggle for the Valley

1 Where and when is the meeting taking place?

2 Why has the Expert come to chair the meeting?

3 What do the members of the Galinsk collective want to use the valley for?

4 What alternative use for the valley do the Rosa Luxemburg fruit farm collective propose?

5 Who is to decide the future of the valley?

6 How does the goatherd use the cheese he passes around to make a point?

7 What does the soldier say about the rights of possession?

8 What does the Girl Tractor Driver say about the law?

9 How does the Peasant Woman explain her opposition to the State?

10 The Expert sums up. What does he say?

11 What is the Agronomist's plan for the valley? (When was the plan devised?)

12 Outline the goatherds' alternative plan.

13 Which plan is accepted?

14 What do you learn about the play which is about to be performed by the fruit farmers?

Scene Two The Noble Child

1 How does the language of the play differ from the language of Scene One?

2 What is Nukha like?

3 What do you learn about the city's Governor, Georgi Abashvili, his family and his style of leadership? What are his main concerns?

4 Does the scene involving the two doctors develop your understanding of the Governor? Is the despatch rider's attempted interruption important?

5 Describe the meeting between Grusha and Simon. Why do they speak to each other in the third person?

6 Why is the Governor suspicious of Prince Kazbeki? How are his suspicions justified?

7 Why must Simon leave? What is Grusha's reaction to his departure? What promises are made?

8 How does the Governor's wife come to leave the child behind?

9 Why does Grusha take the child? What does the Singer mean by, 'terrible is the temptation to do good'? Does anyone support Grusha in her action?

Scene Three The Flight into the Northern Mountains

1 How does the behaviour of the Peasant contrast with Grusha's recent actions?

2 What do you think Brecht is saying about class in the scene where Grusha encounters the 'ladies' at the caravansary?

3 What are your first impressions of the Ironshirts?

4 Why does Grusha leave the baby on the Peasant Woman's doorstep? How does the woman react when she finds the child?

5 Describe Grusha's encounter with the Ironshirts.

6 Why does she go back to the cottage?

7 How does the Peasant Woman support Grusha and the child? How does Grusha escape?

8 At the end of the scene Grusha changes the baby into rags and says, 'I'll wash you and christen you'. Christen the baby into what, do you think?

9 Have Grusha's feelings towards the child developed by the end of this scene? If so, how?

Scene Four In the Northern Mountains

1 How is Grusha received at the home of her brother?

2 What is her strategy for survival?

3 Grusha and the child stay at the house of her brother through the winter, then he begins to worry about the neighbours. Why? What is his plan?

4 In agreeing to Lavrenti's plan, Grusha makes a sacrifice. What?

5 Describe the wedding. Is Brecht making a point in his depiction of this wedding?

6 How does Yussup treat Grusha after their marriage? How does she treat him?

7 Describe Simon's return. What is the Singer's function at this point in the play?

Scene Five The Story of the Judge

1 Describe your reaction to the fact that Brecht leaves the story of Grusha. Can you suggest why he does this?

2 Describe Azdak's encounter with the Grand Duke.

3 How does Azdak become a judge?

4 Describe, with examples, Azdak's approach to his new job.

5 What effect do you think Azdak's judgements have on the poor people?

6 Why does he regret the impending restoration of the Grand Duke?

7 How does Azdak lose his job as a judge? How does he get it back again?

8 How does Azdak behave when Natella Abashvili enters?

Scene Six The Chalk Circle

1 What is Grusha's plan for reclaiming Michael?

2 Why is Natella Abashvili eager to have Michael back?

3 The Singer explains that Grusha does not want Michael to be rich. Why?

4 How does Grusha react to Azdak?

5 What test is set by Azdak?

6 Describe what happens in this test. What is Azdak's judgement?

7 What becomes of Azdak after the trial? How is he remembered?

8 What is the moral pointed out by the Singer? How does this connect with the judgement at the end of Scene One?

2 Explorations

A *Further questions*

1 Grusha's story has been described as a fairy tale. Can you identify any aspects of it which are like a fairy tale?

2 Why do you think Brecht chose to set the first scene of the play in 1944? (In an earlier version of the Prologue he had set the discussion in 1934. He clearly thought, eventually, that 1944 was a more pertinent date.)

3 How is 'justice' arrived at in the first scene? What does this tell you about the world of collective farms in the USSR as Brecht sees them?

4 Critics responded with hostility to the first scene of the play when it was first performed in 1954. Brecht was puzzled: 'That the prologue displeases you I don't quite understand' he said. What do you think the Prologue is *for*? What does it add to Grusha's story?

5 'The judge was always a rascal' says an Ironshirt in Scene Five. What view do you think the poor people of Grusinia have of the law? Why did they hang Judge Orbellani? Who does justice serve in Grusinia?

6 Is Azdak a popular judge with the people? Do they see him as 'different' from earlier judges? If so, how is he different?

7 Brecht said that Azdak, 'continues to practise bourgeois law'. What do you think he meant by this? How is Azdak's justice different from the justice arrived at in Scene One?

8 What view do you think Brecht had of the law in relation to truth? (A clue: Azdak makes 'appropriate' judgements by twisting the law, so what is Brecht saying about the law?)

9 On the surface it might appear that Azdak's courtroom is anarchic and farcical. Do you detect a view of society as it *should* be beneath the comedy?

10 Why do you think Grusha rescues the baby?

11 Brecht did not want the audience to find Grusha glamorous,

especially in the early scenes. How does he attempt to do this? Do you think he succeeds?

12 What does Grusha sacrifice in order to protect the child?

13 Look at Grusha's outburst against Azdak in the final scene. What is Brecht saying about wealth and power through Grusha? (A clue: why does she reject, on Michael's behalf, the opportunity for him to become rich?)

14 Why do you think Brecht uses the Singer to reveal the characters' thoughts, rather than having them tell the audience their thoughts directly?

15 Can you seen any other reasons for Brecht's use of the Singer and Musicians?

B *Assignments*

1 Brecht describes the theatre of his day as 'culinary' – it appealed to the senses but did not stimulate the mind. He wanted theatre to be 'entertaining and at the same time instructive … transformed from a place of illusion to a place of insight.' Brecht's kind of theatre is called 'epic theatre'. In 1930 he tabulated the differences between his 'epic theatre' and the 'dramatic theatre' of his time:

Dramatic Theatre	Epic Theatre
plot	narrative
implicates the spectator in a stage situation	turns the spectator into an observer, but
wears down his capacity for action	arouses his capacity for action
provides him with sensations	forces him to take decisions
experience	picture of the world
the spectator is involved in something	he is made to face something
suggestion	argument
instinctive feelings are preserved	brought to the point of recognition

Dramatic Theatre	Epic Theatre
the spectator is in the thick of it, shares the experience	the spectator stands outside, studies
the human being is taken for granted	the human being is the object of the inquiry
he is unalterable	he is alterable and able to alter
eyes on the finish	eyes on the course
one scene makes another growth	each scene for itself montage
linear development	in curves
man as a fixed point	man as a process
thought determines being	social being determines thought
feeling	reason

(from *Brecht on Theatre*, p. 37)

How does *The Caucasian Chalk Circle* illustrate Brecht's views on theatre?

The following suggestions may help you to prepare your response to this assignment.

1 Look at Grusha's development. How (and why) does she change during the course of the play?

2 What is the Prologue (Scene One) for?

3 How does Brecht use the Singer and Musicians?

4 Why do you think Brecht divides the play into scenes (episodes?) What is the purpose of each scene?

5 Finally, do you think he succeeds in stopping you becoming too emotionally involved? Does he make you think?

2 How is justice achieved in the Prologue to *The Caucasian Chalk Circle*? How does Azdak achieve justice? Identify the differences and similarities between the two versions of justice.

3 Trace Grusha's development from a naive girl to a woman who challenges the honesty of a judge in court.

4 What do you think Brecht intends in his portrayal of Azdak?

5 Compile a design brief for *The Caucasian Chalk Circle*. Describe the set and costumes, and give reasons for choosing the designs you have made. Look at Brecht's ideas on 'epic theatre' before you begin and justify your decisions in relation to his ideas.

6 Describe the roles played by the Singer and the Musicians in *The Caucasian Chalk Circle*.

7 Analyse the effect you think Brecht wanted his play to have upon you.

C *Further Reading*

John Willet, *Brecht in Context*, Methuen, 1984
Peter Demetz (ed.), *Brecht: Critical Essays*, Prentice-Hall, 1987
Bartram and Waine (eds), *Brecht in Perspective*, Longman, 1982
John Willet (ed.), *Bertolt Brecht*, Eyre Methuen, 1964

Other plays by Brecht

Bertolt Brecht, *Mother Courage and her Children*, Methuen
Bertolt Brecht, *The Life of Galileo*, Methuen